AF560143

MUSCULO-SKELETAL DISORDERS
SOCIO-CULTURAL DIMENSIONS

MUSCULO-SKELETAL DISORDERS
SOCIO-CULTURAL DIMENSIONS

By

Dr. Robin D. Tribhuwan
M.A., M.Sc., PGDM, Ph.D.
&
Dr. Satish N. Meshram
MBBS, MS (Orthopaedics)
M.A., MSW, M.A., PGDPH

DISCOVERY PUBLISHING HOUSE PVT. LTD.
NEW DELHI-110 002

Published by:
Tilak Wasan
DISCOVERY PUBLISHING HOUSE PVT. LTD.
4383/4B, Ansari Road, Darya Ganj
New Delhi-110 002 (India)
Phone : +91-11-23279245, 43596064-65
Fax : +91-11-23253475
E-mail : discoverypublishinghouse@gmail.com
sales@discoverypublishinggroup.com
parul.wasan@gmail.com
web : www.discoverypublishinggroup.com

***First Edition:* 2014**

ISBN: 978-93-5056-472-1

Musculo-Skeletal Disorders: *Socio-Cultural Dimensions*

Printed at:
Dynamic Printers
Delhi

Preface

As students of High School, Higher Secondary schools and College, we learn about human body, its anatomy and physiology. We are also taught about the skeletal system and the various bones. However, as time passes by we take a totally different subject for higher studies and professional carrier, and in the process forget about the basics of skeletal system and the bones.

Our revision of the skeletal, system, bones and fractures starts, when someone in our family meets with an accident breaks a bone or becomes a victim of musculo-skeletal injury. Some times, we ourselves become a patient of an orthopedic disorder, we then wake up to know more about the disorder. Some people read books and find information about arthritis, osteoporosis, osteomyelitis or other musculo-skeletal disorders.

What ever information we get about a given musculo-skeletal disorder is either by reading about it or information given by the orthopedic expert or the cultural knowledge about the same passed on to us by the family or village elders by word of mouth, through the oral tradition.

The objective of writing this book is two fold:

1. To create awareness among the readers regarding basic knowledge about the medical interpretation of some of the major musculo-skeletal disorders.
2. Secondly, to unveil the cultural beliefs and practices of people regarding body image its growth and development, people's perception regarding the origin

and cause of a musculoskeletal disorder, the therapies they prefer, the nature and role of traditional bone setters as well as orthopaedic experts, the health seeking behavior of people, the ethno-nutritional beliefs and practices they associate with Orthopaedic treatment and so on.

Interestingly, the book is a combination of the intellectual efforts and research background of two authors from two different academic backgrounds. The first author is a trained Anthropologist, with vast research and several publications in social sciences. While, the second author is an experienced practicing orthopaedic surgeon, with several degrees in social sciences. The facts presented in the book are based on primary and secondary data, on the socio-cultural and medical dimensions of the major musculo-skeletal disorders.

This book will certainly be useful to medical, health and social scientists, researchers, students and general readers. The data on the socio-cultural dimensions of orthopaedic disorders, reported in the book, will be useful to health administrators and policy makers to plan and implement culturally acceptable and economically feasible programs for the diverse ethnic and cultural population of India. It will spark interest among the researchers to carry out research on the beliefs and practices of tribal, caste, nomadic, slum and upper and middle class communities in India on the socio-cultural aspects of orthopedics. The data base of the study will contribute in planning awareness and health education programs for tribal, rural and urban population.

Dr. **Robin D. Tribhuwan**
MA, MSC, PGDM, Ph.D.

Dr. **Satish N. Meshram**
MBBS, MS (Orthopaedics)
MSW, MA, PGDPH

Contents

1

Socio-cultural Dimensions of Musculo-skeletal Disorders *An Insider's View*

THE PURPOSE AND SIGNIFICANCE OF THE BOOK

Inspired by the 100+ book series authored by John Ebnezar on various issues that deal with orthopaedic problems of public health importance, that aimed at educating the readers on scientific and medical aspects of orthopaedics and musculo-skeletal problems and disorders, the authors of this book felt that it is not only necessary to educate the readers, but policy makers, health administrators, medical and paramedical staff, health scientists, public health experts, non-government organisations, social scientists, social orthopaedic surgeons workers and others regarding the social, cultural, educational, economical, and occupational aspects associated with musculo-skeletal disorders and problems.

The subject of musculo-disorders and orthopaedic problems is so vast that one would take decades to document the socio-cultural dimensions of each orthopaedic disorder. We feel that is book is a humble beginning to spark interest among medical health and social scientists to work collectively to understand the perceptions of common people the Tribals, the nomadic communities, the rural inhabitants of India about musculo-skeletal problems and disorders. Dr. Robin D. Tribhuwan, a trained experienced Anthropologist and a hard care field worker, who has authored and edited over 37 books and published over 200 research papers, felt the need and urgency of researching and publishing a book on the socio-cultural dimensions of musculo-skeletal disorders and problems. Dr. Tribhuwan worked with Dr. Satish. N. Meshram, an Orthopaedic surgeon, who has background in social science. Moreover, he has completed, Ph.D., in social work, and has been a practicing orthopaedic surgeon, since 20 years. Both the authors,s are currently working in a Sensitive-Naxal affected district called Gadchiroli, in Maharashtra, India. The authors believe that this combined research effect in the form of this book will help a reader immensely in getting the right knowledge regarding the insider's (common man's) view of musculo-skeletal disorders. It is pertinent to note that very few orthopaedic surgeons are interested to carry out research on socio-cultural aspects of orthopaedics, as they are busy with their practice and consultation, secondly as pointed out rightly by John Ebnezar (2012; i) that most people depend on internet and magazines which distort and misinterpret various pieces of information concerning health topics, leaving the readers confused and still worse improperly educated. The purpose of this book is to spark interest among young research scholars in the field of social, health and medical sciences to work collectively to understand the problems associated with musculo-skeletal disorders as viewed by the common people. We believe that unless and until we understand what people know about orthopaedics, musculo-skeletal problems, and human skeletal system its physiology, anatomy about fractures, strains, sprains etc. We cannot design appropriate health education programmes for them.

The book also aims at creating awareness among the public health care administrators, policy makers and health care providers that the poor tribals, nomadic groups, rural inhabitants, labourers belonging to unorganized sector, people belonging to lower class cannot afford the costly orthopaedic treatment and hence prefer to go to government hospitals, to traditional bone setters, quacks or live with the disability or the said musculo-skeletal problem.

The economics of orthopaedic treatment needs to be collectively researched by medical and social scientists both from insider's as well as outsider's perspective.

1. Should poor people go to traditional bone setters or orthopaedic surgeons?
2. Can they afford to pay for orthopaedic surgeries, hospitalization, medication, physiotherapy and rehabilitation?
3. Do the general hospitals, rural hospitals, municipality hospitals; primary health centers have enough orthopaedic surgeons and medical man power to handle poor people's orthopaedic problems?
4. Are the operation theatres in Government hospitals well equipped?
5. Is it possible to reduce the cost of orthopaedic treatment keeping in view the poor socio-economic background of patients?

Well, these and several other questions that revolve around the concept of economics of orthopaedic treatment, haunt the mind of a democratic citizen and a researcher, If we pledge to uphold the concept of Health For All, by the year 2020, we need to look into this aspect as well.

The World Health Organisation (1948) has therefore defined health as a state of physical, mental, social and spiritual well-being and merely absence of disease. Hence, it is necessary to study musculo-skeletal disorders from a holistic perspective. Medical Anthropologists are trained to understand a given health problem from a holistic perspective.

As aptly pointed out by Hasan K.A (1979) that, medical science has always focused its attention to the study of causative factors in illness and its domain has been in biological and physical science in dealing with problems of health and disease. Man is unique in having cultural environment.

This includes all the conditions in which human beings are born, live, work, procreate and die. Culture as an environment is deeply related with the health of human beings. In fact, Mutatkar R.K, a well known Anthropologist, states that health is an aspect of human culture.

Human cultures everywhere include patterns of social organisation designed to regulate a particular society. The members can understand the behaviour of most people and they can predict how an individual will react in a given situation.

It is therefore, the need of the time for the progressive medical and public health care administrators, workers, policy makers, educators and health care providers, to keep in that culturally determined habits such as the manner of easing, eating, sleeping, working, and social customs and traditions play an important role in control and maintenance of disease. The study of people's beliefs regarding pain, fractures, musculo-skeletal problems and disorders, therapy etc will certainly help the health administrators in framing social policies. Thus, the concept of cultural environment is of great value for public health practitioners and administrators. We hope and pray that this book will be of immense use to researchers, students, health, public health practitioners and general readers as well.

ORTHOPAEDICS: MEDICAL INTERPRETATION

Before getting into the statement of the problem, it is necessary to give the readers a brief understanding about the medical interpretation of orthopaedics. The term orthopaedics has been coined by Nicholas Andry, a French physician, from two words namely ortho – meaning straight and paedics meaning child, in the year 1741.

Ebnezar John (2002) states that the science of Orthopaedics, once upon a time called a primitive branch, then restricted to correcting deformities in children, has now developed into a full-fledged specialty with diverse scope ranging from simple treatment, to highly advanced joint, spine and limb surgeons.

The development of orthopaedics as a speciality was pedestrian till 18th century. The discovery of anesthesia and aseptic surgical techniques opened up new avenues of treatment like open reduction, debridement etc. The discovery of x-rays, and the introduction of the usage of Plaster of Paris by Albert Mathysen in 1852, revolutionized the diagnosis and management of orthopaedic disorders. Thus, orthopaedics started breaking the dead lacks of a crude branch to that of a science. (Ebnezar, 2002:3).

But, what really set the ball rolling was the sudden surge of orthopaedic cases firstly by the two world wars and of late by road traffic accidents, which are on the rise, both in the developed and developing countries.

Polytrauma, multiple fractures, high velocity injuries, severely exposed the limitations of the conventional treatments in orthopaedics, as the fracture patterns were bizarre and complicated. Thus, newer modalities of treatment like improved methods of internal fixation, the A.O. systems, the interlocking nail system, Ilizarov method etc. were introduced in orthopaedic management. Suddenly, orthopaedics was being considered a highly specialized branch with vast scope (Ebnezar John, 2002:3).

There is no doubt that orthopaedics is a vast and highly specialized branch, hence the authors have restricted to unveil the social, cultural, economic, educational, ethical and occupation related aspects of a few musculo-skeletal disorders and problems.

Human Bones, Skeletal System and Fractures: An Etic View

A bone is a specialized connective tissue that gives all important shape to the human body. Bones function to protect vital organs of the body such as heart, lungs, brain support the body and contribute in attachment to the muscles and enable them to act on joints by acting as a lever for their action. Bones are made up of 30 per cent organic material and 70 per cent mineral.

Ebnezar John (2000:14) states that the bones of human skeletal system are 206 in number and are grouped into:

1. **Axial Skeleton** – comprising of the 80 bones of the skull, vertebral column, sternum, ribs, ear ossicles etc.
2. **Appendicular Skeleton** – Comprising of 126 bones of shoulder girdle, upper extremities, hip girdle, lower extremity etc.

Types of Bones

Studies by orthopaedic surgeons revealed that there are five types of bones in the skeletal system namely:

1. **Long bones:** These serve as levers for the muscle action, for example femur, tibia etc.
2. **Short bones:** These are generally cube-shaped and are found in areas where limited movements are required. Their principal role is to provide strength.
3. **Flat bones:** These consists of parallel layers of compact bones separated by a thin layer of bone tissue, for example scapula, skull etc.
4. **Irregular bones:** These have a peculiar and irregular shape and are unique in their appearances and functions, for example pelvic bones.
5. **Sesamoid bones:** These are small, rounded or triangular bones which develop within the substance of a tendon or fascia. Their name is derived from their resemblance with sesame seeds for example, patella.

About Joints

A joint exists where two or more skeletal components – whether bone or cartilage, come together to meet. Without joints in between the bones your body would be rigid and immobile. Ebnezar John (2002:16) has classified joints into three major groups:

1. **Fibrous joints or synarthrosis:** These are immovable joints for example, sutures of the skull.
2. **Cartilaginous joints or amphorthosis:** These are slightly movable joints with either hyaline or fibrous cartilage in between.

3. **Synovial joints and diarthrosis:** These form the majority of the joints in the body. They have between the bones, a synovial or joint cavity. They form the most mobile joints in the body. Some of the examples of synovial joints are:
   - Elbow joints
   - Hip joints
   - Radio carpal joints
   - Knee joints etc.
4. **Fractures:** When a bone breaks it is bound to injure the surrounding soft tissues like muscles, ligaments etc. Given below are definitions of fracture, dislocation, subluxation, sprain, strain and types of fractures etc.

Definitions

1. **Fracture:** A fracture is a break in the surface of the bone, either across its cortex or through its articular surface. Some orthopaedic surgeons define fracture as a break in the continuity.
2. **Dislocation:** Dislocation is a complete and persistent displacement of a joint in which at least part of the supporting joint capsule and some of its ligaments are disrupted.
3. **Subluxation:** Subluxation is a partial dislocation of a joint.
4. **Sprain:** Sprain is a injury of the ligament.
5. **Strain:** Strain is a tear in the muscle.

Types of Fractures

Ebnezar John (2000:17-18) has classified three types of fractures namely:

1. **Simple or compound fractures**

When the bone can break within its soft tissue envelopes and many not communicate to the exterior is known as Simple or Closed Fracture.

When the bone may rip through its soft tissues or the soft tissue itself may be damaged by the external forces, exposing the bone to external atmosphere is known as compound or open fractures.

2. **Based on the extent of fracture line**
   - **Incomplete fractures:** These involve only one surface or cortex of the bone.
   - **Complete fractures:** Here the fractures involve the entire bone. A complete fracture could be undisplaced or displaced.
3. Based on fracture patterns (orthopaedic trauma association classification)
   - **Linear fractures:** These could be transverse, oblique or spiral. Any fracture which forms an angle less than 30° with the horizontal line is called transverse. Angle equal to or more than 30° is termed oblique.
   - **Communicated fractures:** Here the fracture fragments are more than two in number.
   - **Segmental fractures:** A fracture can break into segments, and the segment could be two level, three level, a longitudinal split or communicated.
   - **Bone loss:** This could be a less than 50 per cent bone loss or more than 50 per cent bone loss or complete bone loss.

Examples of Typical Fractures

Some of the typical fractures as classified by orthopaedic experts are:

- **Green stick fractures:** It is seen exclusively among children. Here the bone is elastic and usually binds due to buckling or breaking of one cortex, when a force is applied. This is called a green stick fracture.
- **Impacted fractures:** Here the fracture fragments are impacted into each other and are not separated and displaced.
- **Stress or fatigue fractures:** It is usually an incomplete fracture commonly seen in athletes and in bones subjected to chronic and repetitive stress. (Example: third metatarsal fracture, fracture tibia etc.)
- **Pathological fractures:** It occurs in a diseased bone and usually is spontaneous. The force required to bring out a pathological fracture is trivial.

- **Hairline or crack fracture:** It is a very fine break in the bone, which difficult to diagnose clinically. Radio logically usually helps.
- **Torus Fracture:** This is just a buckling of the outer cortex.

Displacement of Fractures

A complete fracture usually gets displaced due to various factors. Depending on the direction of the force, mode of injury, pull of the muscles, a fracture can show any one of the following displacement or angulations.

1. Anterior angulations or displacement.
2. Posterior angulations or displacement.
3. Medical angulations or displacement.
4. Lateral angulations or displacement.
5. Shortening.
6. Translation.

Deformities

Deformity is defined as any deviation from the normal anatomy of a bone and joint is called a deformity. (Ebnezar John, 2000:21)

Classification of Deformities

Deformities of the skeletal system are classified into two broad categories namely:

1. Deformities since Birth (Congenital)

These deformities are due to some genetic abnormalities or environmental variations or both. They may be obvious at birth or may be seen few years later. Incidence of congenital deformities is up to 2 to 3 per cent.

2. Acquired Deformities

These deformities could be due to problems in the bone, joint or soft tissue. Given below are three major causes of acquired deformities namely:

(a) **Bone Causes**

(i) **Growth Disturbances:** Tumor, infection or trauma near the growth epiphysis can cause either unequal

stimulus, suppressions or stimulation of growth. This results in bending, shortening or lengthening of a bone respectively for example; osteomyelitis, epiphytical injuries, tumor etc.

(ii) **Bone Disorders:** Endocrine disorders, metabolic disorders, developmental disorders are some of the examples of bone disorders.

(iii) **Fractures:** This is by far the most important cause for deformity. All displaced and fresh fractures cause temporary deformity, while mal-union or non-union of fractures lead to deformities at later date.

(b) **Joint Causes:** The causes for the deformities to joint are varied. Given below are few examples.

(i) **Dislocation or Subluxation:** This is usually due to trauma. It may be seen due to pathological conditions of the hip. For example; T.B. hip.

(ii) **Muscle Misbalance:** Muscles balancing the joint or either side, if they are either over active (for example; cerebral palsy) or under active for example; polio, deformity of the joint results.

(iii) **Tethering of Muscles and Tendons:** This can take place due to growth of fibrous tissue following infections or due to callus following fractures. Tethering restricts the joint movement and if it is held for some time definitely results for example; VIC, Tenosynovitis of finger flexes etc.

(iv) **Arthritis** of any joint may give rise to muscle spasm in the initial stages and fibrous in later stages giving rise to deformities, for example; T.B. knee, rheumatoid hand, T.B. hip etc.

(v) **Postural:** This is due to improper postural habits in women due to tight and rigid shoes.

(vi) **Idiopathic:** Here there is no apparent cause for the joint deformities for example; idiopathic scoliosis.

(c) **Deformity Due to Soft Tissue Contract:** Soft tissue contractures (skin and deep fascia) other than the muscle contractures can also cause joint deformities for example; Dupuytron's contractures, post burn contractures etc. The subject of orthopaedic disorders is a vast field, we have therefore restricted ourselves to understanding socio-cultural diversities of a few.

(i) **Musculo-Skeletal Disorders:** But before getting into it let us briefly explain what musculo-disorders & problems are.

Musculo-Skeletal Disorders and Problems

Musculo-skeletal disorders and problems can be defined as those disorders of the muscles, bones, joints and skeletal system, that are congenital (by birth) or acquired. These encompass a wide range of problems starting from bones, muscles, joint injuries, strains, sprains and damages associated with neuro-vascular structures. Given below is a broad classification of orhtopaedic disorders and problems as given by Suryabhan (1993); Ebnezar John (2000); Kumar Abhishek (2010).

This broad classification is as given below:

I. **General Orthopaedics:** This includes following musculo-skeletal disorders and problems:

1. Congenital disorders
2. Development disorders
3. Unclassified disorders
4. Infections of the bones
5. Diseases of the joints
6. Bone tumours
7. Metabolic diseases of the bones
8. Neurological disorders
9. Disorders of the peripheral nerves
10. Leg length inequality and amputations

II. **Regional Orthopaedics:** This includes following musculo-skeletal disorders and problems:

1. Hip related musculo-skeletal disorders and problems.
2. Knee related musculo-skeletal disorders and problems.

3. Ankle & foot related musculo-skeletal disorders and problems.
4. Shoulder related musculo-skeletal disorders and problems.
5. Elbow related musculo-skeletal disorders and problems.
6. Wrist related musculo-skeletal disorders and problems.
7. Hand related musculo-skeletal disorders and problems.
8. Neck related musculo-skeletal disorders and problems.
9. Spine related musculo-skeletal disorders and problems.

III. **Individual Fractures & Injuries**

1. Injuries of the shoulder and arm
2. Injuries of the elbow and fore arm
3. Injuries of the wrist and hand
4. Injuries of the pelvis
5. Injuries of the knee and leg
6. Injuries of the ankle and foot
7. Injuries of the spine and paraplegia
8. Ligament injuries
9. Stress fractures
10. Paediatric injuries
11. Pathological fractures

Further, Babhulkar Sudhir (1997) an eminent orthopaedic surgeon, has revealed that out of the 7380 patients of sickle cell haemoglobinopathies diagnosed and followed up by him from 1-1-1970 to 31-12-1995 in various camps and OPD's of Vidarbha region, 944 patients suffered from skeletal manifestations. This means that almost 13 per cent sickle cell patients developed skeletal manifestations and bone changes.

Dr. Satish Meshram's study (2012) revealed that 15 per cent of the sickle cell patients diagnosed by him, suffered from skeletal manifestations and bone changes and were physical disabled. He studied the socio-cultural and medical aspects associated with the 15 per cent patients studied by him. Sickle cell disease also leads to skeletal manifestations and bone changes and hence is a research problem.

STATEMENT OF THE PROBLEM

The Processes of technological advancement, globalization, urbanization, modernization and planned development has been responsible for creating several occupations groups and job opportunities. These processes have also been instrumental for fast, busy and complicated life styles. Modern livelihood depends a lot on how much one earns within short time. There is struggle and competition in the 21st century for survival. People travel to long distances for jobs either by public transport or own vehicle. In India, people belonging to middle and lower classes prefer to buy two wheelers, because they are cheap and easy to maintain. The rapid increase in production and use of two wheelers and four wheelers has been one of the fundamental cause of accidents.

Similarly, the different types of occupational groups in the unorganized or informal sector are at a higher risk to injuries and accidents. Some of these occupational groups are the stone quarry workers, construction labourers, painters, scrap collectors, sand workers, salt pan workers, sugarcane cutters, wood cutters, minor forest collectors, electricians, agriculture labourers etc.

A World Health Organisations publication captioned, "Injuries and violence: The Facts" (2010) reveals that, all the deaths worldwide. It states that one dies from an injury every five seconds. More than 15,000 people die as a result of injuries every day. About 5.8 million people die of injuries every year. Further, one quarter (23%) of the 5.8 million deaths each year are the result of road traffic crashes which represent the single leading cause of injury related deaths.

1. Trends, Causes and Indices of Injury Related Deaths

According to yet another WHO's publication in collaboration with the Education Development Centre (2010), leading causes of death from injuries, ie; road traffic crashes, are expected to be among the top leading causes of death in the world by 2030. In fact road traffic crashes are predicted to become fifth leading cause of death by 2030.

This publication has also highlighted the risk age groups that become victims of injuries. It states that injuries are one of the top three causes of death among people between the ages of 5 and 44 years. Road traffic injuries are the leading cause of deaths for young people between 15 and 29 years of age.

Further, nearly twice as many men as women die of injuries each year. Within countries, poorer people have higher rates of injury-related deaths than wealthier people. More than 90 per cent of injury-related deaths occur in low and middle income countries. Injury death rates are higher in poorer countries than in high income countries in all the regions of the world.

One of the major issue related to injuries in the economic cost of treatment. The World Report on Road Traffic Injury Prevention published by the World Health Organisation (2004) states that, along with the significant – and the devastating – physical, mental, and emotional consequences of injuries, those affected often experience considerable economic losses resulting from:

- Cost of treatment, including incident investigation and rehabilitation.
- Reduced or lost productivity (i.e; in wages).

It is pertinent to note that road crashes cost most countries between 1 to 2 per cent of their gross national product. The economic cost of road traffic crashes worldwide has been estimated at US $ 518 billion. Well given above are statistics related to injuries and road crashes. However, it is a naked truth that accidents, injuries, fractures that occur among occupational groups working in the informal sector or unorganized sector are not accounted for. There may be few exceptions.

Given below is a table 1.1 that shows occupational groups in unorganized sector and causes of injuries, fractures, sprains, swellings and other musculo-skeletal disorders and problems.

Table 1.1: Table Depicting Occupational Groups and Musculo-Skeletal Problems

Sr. No.	Occupational Group	Musculo-Skeletal Problem
1.	Stone Quarry Workers	Fractures, injuries, swellings, sprains, backache etc due to landslides, a stone falling on the body, injuries while cutting or breaking the stone and so on.
2.	Sugarcane Cutters	While cutting sugarcane, accidentally a finger, palm, flesh or bone gets deeply or fully cut, thereby creating physical pain, mental and emotional problems to the patient.
3.	Construction Labourers	Fractures and injuries due to fall from a multi-storyed building.
4.	Painters	Fractures and injuries caused due to fall while painting.
5.	Coal Mine Workers & Labourers	Fractures and injuries caused due to blasts at work sites.
6.	Wood Cutters	Injuries & fractures caused while cutting word or a fall from the tree.
7.	Tendu Leaf & Honey Gatherers	Fall from the tree may cause fracture, sprain, swelling or injury.
8.	Coolies who Carry Grain Bags	Spine related fractures or problems are common among coolies who carry heavy weight grain bags on their backs.

Well, one can go on with classifying injuries, accidents, fractures, sprains and swellings caused to labourers and their children belonging to the unorganized sector. It is necessary to maintain records of the accidents and injuries that occur among the above mentioned and several other neglected occupational groups belonging to the unorganized sector.

Tribhuwan Robin & Jayshree Patil (2009) have highlighted health problems of the stone quarry workers; Tribhuwan Robin & Shende Sadashiv (2012) have thrown light on the health issues of salt pan workers of Gujarat; Tribhuwan Robin & Kharche J. (2012) have thrown light on the health hazards of brick kiln labourers and sugarcane cutters.

In his book captioned, "Yoga therapy for low backache", Ebnezar John (2012) has classified four classes of occupational groups namely:

1. **The Upper Group:** This group includes professionals like bureaucrats, politicians, managers, secretaries and top executives.
2. **The Middle Group:** This group includes the clerks, assistants, typists, stenographers, secretaries etc.
3. **The Lower Group:** To this group belong the peons, attendants, office boys, watchman, security guards, cleaners, scavengers etc.
4. **Special Group:** This group includes doctors, computer engineers, policemen, soldiers, sports persons, athletes etc.

Ebnezar John (2012) has shown the variations of backache problems among the above mentioned professionals and workers. He has clearly pointed out the co-relation between backache, people's habits, life styles, work culture and occupational profession. In the same book, he writes that backache is a worldwide problem. 8 out of 10 people are affected with backache at some or the other stage of life. It is next only to common cold and headache.

2. Etiology of Musculo-Skeletal Disorders

Yet another research problem that is associated with musculo-skeletal disorders is people's perception regarding the origin and cause of these disorders, which is culturally determined. People's etiology of musculo-skeletal disorders is different from the scientific and medical interpretation of the origin and cause of the disorder. Medical doctors need to understand the socio-cultural dimensions of musculo-skeletal disorders.

3. Health Expenditure

People who suffer from musculo-skeletal disorders and problems not only become victims of the devastating physical, mental and emotional consequences of injuries but also experience considerable economic losses resulting from cost of treatment, hospitalization, medication, physiotherapy and rehabilitation.

We have reported cases studies of patients who borrowed many on heavy interest from money lenders, a few took loan from friends and relatives and some sold their agriculture land and property. It was observed that economic loss in an additional psychological pressure and stress to the parents, spouses and family members of the patient. Economic loss in orthopaedic treatment is yet another research problem.

4. Additional Responsibility and Extra Care

The parents, spouses, kins and family members are burdened with additional responsibility to take care of the patient suffering from a given musculo-skeletal disorder. At times working parents have to hire services of a nurse or maid to take care of their child suffering from an orthopaedic problem. If elderly people are patients, their working children cannot be with them full time. This creates misunderstanding between them and gives rise to quarrels. Well, this is yet another research problem.

5. Physical Disability, Trauma and Social Stigma

Patients who become physically disabled due to injuries or amputation suffer from psychological trauma and social stigma. Young boys and girls whose hands or legs get amputed are stressed and get worried. Some of the questions that worry them are:

- I am physically handicapped person.
- Will I get married?
- What is my status in the family, community & in the society?
- Will I get a job?
- Am I a burden to my spouse, parents & family members?
- Am I unlucky?
- Have I committed sins in the past or present life, that I have to become a handicapped person?
- Why did god do this to me?

This is yet another research problem associated with musculo-skeletal disorders and problems.

6. Ethno-nutritional Beliefs

Studies by Ethnographers and Anthropologists have documented people's beliefs regarding the impact of food, water, milk, juices, meat etc on anatomy and physiology of human body. In this book an attempt has been made to unveil people's beliefs regarding foods that strengthen bones, join bones, make muscles strong. There is an urgent need to research concept of ethno-nutritional beliefs and practices of people associated with musculo-skeletal disorders.

7. Medical Ethics in Orthopaedics

It is a well known fact that, orthopaedic treatment is costly. Secondly, it is a established fact that people who belong to the lower income groups cannot afford take treatment in private orthopaedic hospitals and institutions. Thirdly, patients and their family members are unaware of the cost and quality of implants that are used by the orthopaedic surgeons. There are cases where the rates of the implants have been increased two to three times than the actual cost of the implants. The patients get taxed economically due to lack of awareness regarding the rates of implants, fees and consultation of the orthopaedic surgeon, fees of physiotherapists, hospitalization and rehabilitation. The significance of medical ethics, transparency and accountability plays an important role in doctor-patient relationship and transactions. Medical ethics in orthopaedics is hence an important research problem that needs to be probed.

8. Why Poor People Prefer Traditional Bone Setters?

Poor people cannot afford the costly treatment in private orthopaedic hospitals because some of them cannot afford the treatment in government hospitals too, as they have to pay for implants medicine and transportation and hence prefer to go to thebone setters. The traditional bone setters charge reasonable amount from Rs. 30/- to Rs. 500/- as the case may be. Some bone setters take food grains, liquor, coconut, hen etc for their services. While, some don't charge a single penny. That is why poor people, especially in tribal and rural areas prefer to go to traditional bone setters.

Should the traditional bone setters be streamlined in primary health care? Well, this is an area of debate as well as research. The orthopaedic surgeons will certainly oppose this idea, because the diagnosis and treatment methods of traditional bone setters are not scientific. There is a school of thought that supports the main streaming of traditional midwives, herbalists and bone setters, in primary health care.

9. Why People Shift from One Therapy to Another?

During our visits to several traditional bone setters in the rural and tribal areas, it was observed that patients shift from one type of therapy to another. Patients treated or those getting treatment from an orthopaedic surgeon, go to the traditional bone setter. Similarly, those taking treatment from the bone setters shift to allopathic treatment. This shift in treatment is observed among patients suffering from musculo-skeletal disorders. There is a need to conduct research in this area as well.

THEORETICAL CONSIDERATIONS

Social facts are considered to be empirically observable realities. Summation of social facts contributes to formation of a concept. Summation and scientific validation of concepts contributes to formulation of a theory. A theory, be it social science or pure science guides, identification and validation of facts. In this section of the book broad theoretical concepts associated with human health, disease, illness and more precisely with musculo-skeletal disorders and problems are considered. An attempt has been made by the authors to show the variations in interpretation of a few musculo-skeletal disorders and problems as viewed by the medical experts (outsiders view) as well as social scientists and people (insiders) view.

1. Concept of Health as per W.H.O

The World Health Organisation has presented a holistic concept of human health by considering not only physical aspect, but the mental, social and spiritual dimensions as well. Hence, as rightly pointed out by Tribhuwan Robin & Gambhir R.D. (1995:61), that Anthropological interest in medicine, stems from the fact that health and disease, though biological in nature are defined and interpreted culturally as they are related to people's social belief system. Hence, musculo-skeletal disorders and problems are no exception to the above mentioned rule.

2. Concept of Disease, Etiology

Allan Young (1982) in his paper captioned, "Anthropology of illness and sickness defined disease, illness and sickness and pointed out how people's perceptions regarding disease etiology and disease classification are different from that of medical interpretation.

Foster George (1953), (1967), (1983); Lieban Richard (1973); Hasan K.A (1967); Turner Victor (1967); Tribhuwan Robin & Gambhir R.D (1995); Tribhuwan Robin (1998); Jain N.S & Tribhuwan Robin (1996) and Shutlur Mary (1979) have in their studies highlighted how people associate the origin and cause of illness to following factors:

1. Possession of evil spirits.
2. Sexual intercourse with evil spirits.
3. Sexual intercourse with menstruating women.

4. Evil eye.
5. Witchcraft and sorcery.
6. Disruption of human relationships with evil spirits, ancestral spirits, deities, cosmic forces, social groups, relatives etc.
7. Wrath of gods & goddesses.
8. Sins in past birth.
9. Breach of a cultural taboo.
10. Failure to perform a divine duty.
11. Wrath of ancestral spirits.
12. Wrong combination of food.
13. Influence of hot and cold food, air, water & atmosphere.
14. Loss of bodily equilibrium.

3. Disease classification

Tribhuwan Robin (1998) has stated that a disease may be classified differently by a tribe based on the bodily symptoms, colour of blood, bodily fluids, colour of eyes, skin, tongue etc. For example; the term for stool in North India is dûst (stool). Diarrhoea is hence classified on the basis of the colour of the stool, namely "Hara dust" (green stool), "Pila dust" (yellow stool), Lal dust (red stool), and "kala dust" (black stool).

Orthopaedic surgeons classify fractures of bones into several categories such as transverse, oblique, spiral, segmental etc fractures. So also people classify diseases and problems of musculo-skeletal disorders differently.

For example, the traditional bone setters in rural and tribal areas of India, classify fractures on the basis of swelling, the pain experienced by the patient, the size of the swelling, the colour of the skin, the damage of muscles, the gravity and intensity of injury, wound or cut etc. Hence, there is a difference between medical interpretation of classification of musculo-skeletal disorders and people's (insider's) perceptions of classification of the same.

4. Musculo-Skeletal therapy: emic concepts

Studies by Foster G.M (1953), (1967), (1983), Lieban Richard (1973), Turner Victor (1967), Tribhuwan Robin (1995), (1998) have revealed that the decision to choose a therapy largely depends on people's perception of the origin and cause of illness; and their socio-economic and educational background. Primary data gathered by the authors in this book reveals that socio-economic condition along with other factors plays an important role in choosing a therapy to cure musculo-skeletal disorders.

This aspect of economics of musculo-skeletal therapy has been discussed in detail by the authors in a separate chapter.

Lieban Richard (1973) has classified ethno-medical therapy into three categories namely:

1. Herbal therapy or chemo-therapy;
2. Mechanical therapy; and
3. Magico-religious therapy.

Tribhuwan Robin and Gambhir R.D (1995) and Tribhuwan Robin (1998), have given illustrations and examples of the above mentioned therapies, by stating that herbal therapy involves administration of herbal medicines, mechanical therapy involves massage, bone setting, healing swellings, branding technique etc, and magico-religious therapy involves healing rituals. One of the objectives of this book is to show how people consider traditional therapies to cure musculo-skeletal disorders.

5. Nature and Role of Bone Setters

Traditional bone setters have been serving people in their respective societies and regions for ages. Even now, in rural and tribal areas poor people prefer to go to traditional bone setters as they cannot afford to pay for X-rays, MRI, orthopaedic surgery, medicine, hospitalization, physiotherapy and rehabilitation.

Traditional bone setters set bones using conventional methods based on trial & error. They have skills of massage and administer herbal medicines as well. They advise their patients on appropriate diet for healing and joining of bones. They practice to serve people. Tribhuwan Robin's (1998) study reveals that the role of traditional bone setters and other ethno-medical specialists is sanctioned by divine beings and forces.

6. Nature and Role of Orthopaedic Surgeons

John Ebnezar (2012) an orthopaedic surgeon has highlighted the nature and role of orthopaedic surgeons in several of his publications. An orthopaedic surgeon's role to a common man, is that of a health service and health care provider.

People look upon an orthopaedic surgeon as an expert and specialist in orthopaedic disorders and surgeries. This study reveals that there is a lot of difference in the nature and role of a government orthopaedic surgeon and a private practitioner or consultant.

7. Economics of Orthopaedic Treatment

The social model of health is expressed with reference to the World Health Organisation's definition. This study also follows the health belief model. It postulates that people's behaviour in relation to health is related to their perception of the severity of illness, their susceptibility to it and the costs and benefits incurred in following a particular cause of action (Rosenstock 1966, Becker 1974). The model holds that socio-demographic, social and psychological factors are likely to modify health beliefs.

The World Report on Road Traffic Injury & Prevention by the World Health Organisation (2004) states that along with the significant – and often devastating – physical, mental, and emotional consequences of injuries, those affected often experience considerable economic losses from:

- Cost of treatment, including incident investigation and rehabilitation.
- Reduced or lost productivity (ie; in wages), for those disabled or killed by their injuries, and for family members who take time off to care for the injured.

This book throws light on the economics of orthopaedic treatment as observed among the tribals, poor caste societies, the middle class as well as the rich people. The study highlights the health expenditure incurred by various occupational groups both from unorganized or organized sectors. Not much research has been conducted on the economics of orthopaedic treatment.

8. People's Habits, Life Styles, Work Culture and Backache

Studies on occupational health by social scientists, medical and health experts have pointed out the impact of work culture, type of occupations, working conditions etc on the health of staff, officers, workers and labourers.

Sociological studies by Breman Jan and Das Arvind (2000); Breman Jan (1996); Panjiar Smita (2007); Breman Jan (1994); Kendre Balaji (2009); Patnaik Renuka (1996); Tribhuwan Robin & Patil Jayshree (2009); Tribhuwan Robin & Shende Sadashiv (2011); Tribhuwan Robin & Kharche Jayshree (2011); Khatare Akrami (2012) & Ebnezar John (2012) have highlighted the working conditions and environment in which various occupational groups work and the health problems they face.

The study has highlighted case studies and examples of various occupational groups, especially those working in the unorganized sector, that become victims of various musculo-skeletal disorders. Some of the theoretical and practical issues that need to be addressed and need further research are:

1. A survey of injuries, accidents and musculo-skeletal disorders and problems among different occupational groups in the unorganized sector.
2. A detailed documentation of the social, financial and medical security to occupational groups in unorganized sector.
3. Occupation and profession wise musculo-skeletal disorders and problems faced by people.

9. Stress Fractures and Occupational Health

Ebnezar John (2000) defines stress or fatigue fractures as those incomplete fractures, commonly seen among athletes and bones subjected to chronic and repetitive stress. (ie; third metatarsal fracture, fracture of tibia etc).

He further points out that occupational groups and professionals such as traffic police, guards, watchmen, soldiers, sportsmen, athletes etc are high risk groups of stress fractures. It may be therefore concluded that stress fractures are related to people's occupation and profession.

10. Income, Class and Musculo-Skeletal Disorders, Problems and Injuries

World Health Report on Road Traffic Injury Prevention (2004); another report by W.H.O on Injuries and Violence: The Facts (2010); The Journal of Trauma (1998); Societal response to Injury – A WHO publication (2010); Ebnezar John's books (2000) & (2012) have pointed out the co-relation of income and class associated with few musculo – skeletal disorders. This book of ours has thrown light on few case studies and examples. However, more detailed documentation and interdisciplinary research needs to be conducted in this area.

11. Response of Family to Musculo-Skeletal Disorders and Patients

Family is the most basic social institution of a human society. It is formed through the institution of marriage. Some of the basic functions of a family are procreation, enculturation, socialization, education, child rearing etc. Care of the sick is yet another important function performed by a family.

An healthy child brings joy and happiness to the family, where as a sick, physically challenged or mentally challenged child needs extra love and care. In a traditional joint family elders take care of the sick, physically and mentally challenged, elderly persons and even normal members. A nuclear family on the other hand finds it difficult to do so and hence transfer the burden of caring to the secondary institutions, such as day care centers, crèches, old age homes, orphanages, boarding schools, hospitals, rehabilitation centers etc. The problem of caring for the sick as well as children is much more severe among working couples.

The degree of negligence of the physically disabled people in nuclear families, especially among families where in both the spouses are working in higher as compared to other nuclear families. In the present study, it was observed that the patients with musculo-skeletal disorders are psychologically depressed and get neglected. They develop an inferiority complex and feel insecure, in their own family.

Their children and other family members do not like to reveal that they are related to them. Patients with physical disability (amputation), paralysis, manifestations and bone changes due to sickle cell disease feel they are a burden to their family members.

Musculo-skeletal disorders that have direct impact on the original body form, shape, size and beauty creates worries and depression among parents who have such children. Children with amputated forearm, leg, palm, etc are dependent on parents and their siblings. Parents get more worried of daughters with physical disabilities. Who will marry our daughter? Who will give her job? Who will feed her? What will happen to her after we die? These and several other questions disturb them.

Care of patients with physical disability is thus a great concern to a family. Response to physical disability of skeletal system or muscles varies from one family to another.

Rich families can afford to hire services of a full time Doctor, Nurse, A.N.M or an attendant to take care of the patient with amputation, or other musculo-skeletal disability. In fact there are rich people who can afford to create a mini-hospital or special ward within their house, for patients with physical disability. Poor people on the other hand are force to send such people to beg, as they cannot afford to take care of these patients. Some of these patients have to work to earn their livelihood, due to pressure from family elders.

Tribhuwan Robin (1998) and Chapekar L.N (1961) have revealed that the Thakurs of Sahyadri believe that children born with polydactyl are considered to be children of "Khais" – an evil spirit. Such children are neglected after birth and the result is they die.

However, there are societies in India, especially in Gujarat, where in polydactyl is believed to bring good luck. The disease is genetic as well as musculo-skeletal. Thus, a family may respond positively or negatively to patients with musculo-skeletal disorders and problems.

12. Gender Differences, Healthcare and Socialization

It is pertinent to note at this juncture, that in societies where the status of a woman is low, female patients with physical disability are neglected and not much cared for, as compared to normal females.

Psychoanalytic feminism is based on Sigmund Freud's psychoanalytic theories. It maintains that gender is not biological, but is based on psycho-sexual development of the individual. Psychoanalytic feminist believe that gender inequality comes from early childhood experiences, which lead men to believe them to be masculine and women to believe themselves feminine. It is further maintained that gender leads to a social system that is dominated by males, which in turn influences the psycho-sexual development.

Sexism is perpetuated by systems of patriarchy, male dominated social structures leading to the oppression of women. Patriarchy by definition, exhibits male centered norms operating throughout all social institutions that become the standard to which all persons adhere. The contemporary acceptance of gender as a legitimate area of study in the sociology of health and illness, belies a hard fought and ongoing battle for recognition.

Sociologists and other social scientists generally attribute many of behavioural differences between genders to socialization. Socialization is the process of transferring norms, values, beliefs and behaviour to future group members. Gender refers to those social, cultural and psychological traits linked with males and females through particular social contexts. Sex makes us male or female; gender makes us masculine or feminine.

In fact preparations for gender socialization begin even before the birth of a child. One of the first questions people ask of expectant parents is the sex of the child. This is the beginning of a social categorization process that continues throughout life. It is important to keep in mind that gender differences are a combination of social and biological forces; sometimes one or the other has a greater influence, but both play a role in dictating behaviour.

As regards to the response of family to musculo-skeletal disorders and patients some of the theoretical issues that crop up are:

13. Healthcare of Patients Among Working Couples in Nuclear and Joint Families

(a) Are working couples able to take care of their children or parents with physical disability, osteoporosis, amputated limbs, bone infections, severe fractures, etc?

(b) Do patients suffering from above mentioned disorders from the poor families having working couples get neglected due to poor socio-economic background of the family?

(c) Is there gender discrimination of healthcare of patients among working couples in nuclear families?

(d) Are patients of the above mentioned disorders rehabilitated in old age homes, day care centers, hospitals or rehabilitation centers, due to busy schedule of the working couples?

(e) Do rich people and celebrities hire services of orthopaedic surgeons, doctors, nurses and attendants to take of patients with severe musculo-skeletal problems in their family?

(f) Are adopted children, children of step mother or father, second wife or husband with orthopaedic disorders ill-treated as regard health care is concerned?

(g) Do patients suffering from orthopaedic disorders get good treatment and better healthcare in joint families?

In their book captioned, "A text book of social and preventive medicine", Park and Park (1991: 295) have stated that the institution of family is as old as man himself. It is the most basic social cell. The need for its discipline has recently dawned because of the changing social and cultural patterns in the work – and above all of what might be called "quality of life" criteria. The role of family in giving quality health service to victims of musculo-skeletal victims vary as their standard of living differ from each other. There is a need to conduct more research in this area.

14. Societal response to Musculo-Disorders and problems

A society is a group of people, who adhere to a commonly and historically developed, learnt and shared cultural behaviour. Disease etiology concepts vary from one society to another. Physically disabled people having certain severe deformities cannot perform normal functions in the family and also in their occupational set up. The society hence looks upon them differently and responds differently.

A normal boy or a girl would not like to get married to physically disabled person. A physically disabled person develops an inferiority complex, gets neglected, and at times is stigmatized socially. The friend circle and social intercourse of most physically disabled persons is limited.

There are hardly any studies on the societal response to musculo-skeletal disorders, problems and patients. This study has made an attempt to throw light on this aspect keeping in view few musculo-skeletal disorders and problems. There is an urgent need to conduct in-depth interdisciplinary studies on several musculo-skeletal disorders.

Some of the theoretical issues that need attention with reference to above mentioned topic are:

1. What is the societal response to patients having musculo-skeletal disorders?
2. What is the perception of various tribal, nomadic and caste societies in India, regarding origin, cause, disease classification and health seeking behaviour with reference to various musculo-skeletal disorders?

15. Are Musculo-Skeletal Disorders: Social Problems

G.R. Madan (1982) in his two volumes on, "Indian Social Problems", has classified physical disability as one of the social problems. Since physically disabled people cannot perform normal household and occupational duties, the state has made certain constitutional and schematic provisions to safeguard the interests of such persons.

Both government and corporate employees, who become victims of injuries, road crashes or accidents while on duty get their due financial, social security and medical compensations. These provisions are however not there for poor employees belonging to various occupational groups in unorganized or informal sector.

Health safety, financial security, hospitalization and rehabilitation insecurity of labourers such as construction workers, stone quarry workers, coal mine labourers etc is certainly a social problem. Some of the theoretical issues that need further research in this area are:

1. Which musculo-skeletal disorders are social problems in the Indian Social System?
2. How does the Indian Social System, the central and respective state governments respond or cope up with problems associated with musculo-skeletal disorders and problems.
3. What are the constitutional and schematic provisions to safeguard the interests of victims of musculo-skeletal disorders?

16. Body Image, Growth of Bones, Muscles and Skeletal System: Ethno-nutritional Beliefs

People everywhere, have beliefs about body image and symbolism. Based on the knowledge their ancestors have passed on to them through oral tradition, people practice norms related to growth and strengthening of the bones, skeletal system, muscles, various organs and bodily systems. Ethno-nutrition refers to people's beliefs and practices regarding the impact of nutrition on human body. They classify different types of food and consume in various healthy and unhealthy situation.

Studies by Turner Victor (1967); Mary Douglas (1970); Munn Nancy (1973) ; Tribhuwan Robin (1998) revealed that human body becomes a social, divine, supernatural, ancestral, cosmic and natural symbol in certain ritual healing contexts.

17. Foucault's Sociology of Health

Foucault's analysis of modern society moves around the three inter-related aspects of the body, power and knowledge. According to him body is both the target of, and is constituted by, the power relations focused on it, which render obedient and docile. These power relations focused are not external forces but internalized, 'self control'. Foucault argues that body is a transient of social and cultural artifact, and not a part of nature. He further argues that the crucial concepts of the body and disease must be seen as historical products.

The dichotomy of the body as physical reality and body as a metaphor is broken in the analysis of the body as language and both its reality are metaphorical accomplishment. The physical body does not exist without metaphorical accomplishments. Thus, it has been noted that the concepts of body act as political, social and ideological resources in society – the image of the body shapes our understanding of society and understanding of the society shapes our understanding of body. [Foucault, M (1967); (1973); (1976); (1977 a); (1977 b); (1982)]

For example the Thankur's of Sahyadri co-relate the nine bodily openings namely eyes, nostrils, ears, mouth, sternum, naval opening, urethral/vaginal opening, anal and the secret opening to the nine planets in the cosmos. Tribhuwan Robin (1998) Thakurss believe that human body is nothing but a symbol of cosmos. An ideal body has form and hence it is disease and illness free. Free from natural, human, supernatural, ancestral, cosmic and evil pathogenic agents and forces.

Since body is connected with cosmos, the planetary female spirits (Mothya Baya) come to visit a person (human body) during small pox or chicken pox. Visitation of their goddesses or planetary female spirits is considered to be auspicious and hence the Thakur's of Sahyadri perform healing rites by inviting a Shaman (Bhagat), to please the "Mothya Baya", during the state of ill-health. No allopathic medicine, injection or tablet is given to the patient. In fact giving allopathic medicine is a breach of taboo, for it is believed that it may initiate anger among the Mothyabaya. Thus, during the period when a person is visited by Mothya Baya, his/her body becomes a symbol of cosmos.

This study has reported cases of fractures, sprains, bone infection, bone tumor, fall from a tree to wrath of gods and goddesses, black magic, evil eye etc. Further, the study also reported people's perceptions regarding growth and development human bones, muscles and skeletal system.

Efforts have been made by the authors to document foods and medicines that heal fractures, strengthen bones, muscles and skeletal system as named by tribals as well as non- tribals. There is an urgent need to promote and carry out community wise documentation of people's ethno-nutritional beliefs and practices.

18. The Institution of Medicine: Medical and Social Interpretation

The history of medicine is, in fact, the history of humanity itself, with its ups and downs, its brave aspirations after truth and finality, it's pathetic failures. The subject may be treated variously as pageant, an array of books, a procession of characters, a succession of theories, an exposition of human ineptitudes, or as the very bone and marrow of cultural history. As Mathew Arnold said the Acta Sanctorum, "All human life is there". (Fielding Garrison, 1931)

The Oxford Dictionary defines, "Medicine", as an art of healing. The institution of medicine is as old as mankind. Caudil William (1955:721) states that disease has been one of the fundamental problems faced by every human society and every known society has developed ways and means to cope up with it, thereby creating a system of medicine.

Tribhuwan Robin (1998:9) states that the institution of medicine may be interpreted from two aspects namely:

1. **Biomedical:** Which interprets disease and its treatment on germ theory lines.
2. **Socio-cultural:** Which interprets disease etiology to interference of natural, social, spiritual, cosmic, supernatural, evil, ancestral etc.

Pathogenic agents/forces that enter in human body and are either driven away or pleased ritually with the help of a Shamam or specialized medical specialists.

According to the second interpretation the reaction of an ill person may express his work views and important cultural views of his society (Clark, 1959). The relationship of medicine and rest of the culture has been noted by Ackernecht (1942), who said, "medicine is no where independent and following its own motivations. Its character and dynamism dependency on the place it takes in every cultural pattern, they depend on the pattern itself.

The studies by early pioneering social scientists in the field of medicine did give new theoretical dimensions to ethno-medical studies. Some of these studies are as follows:

Mead and Henry (1949) have discussed the general relationship of Anthropology with psycho-somatic medicine, Hall (1951) has outlined the progress of sociological research in the field of medicine; outstanding over the years is the classic statement by W.H.R. Rivers (1924) which gives the relationship between religion, magic and medicine; and Clements work tracing the world-wide distribution of five basic categories of disease, attributed to sorcery, breach of taboo, object intrusion, spirit intrusion and loss of soul. (Clement, 1932).

(a) Definition of Ethno-Medicine

The term ethno-medicine is used to refer to those beliefs and practices relating to health and disease, which are products of indigenous cultural development and are not explicitly derived from the conceptual framework of modern medicine. (Hughes Charles 1968:99)

Tribhuwan Robin (1998: 23) has defined ethno-medicine as a culturally ordered inter-relationship of medical symbols and meanings that are associated with a community's notions of illness ideology, body image and the entire set of preventive, promotive and curative health rituals and/or actions performed by the participant actors in various healing contexts, as a symbolic system, which represents the cultural whole.

(b) Areas of Ethno-Medicine

The subject of ethno-medicine focuses on the nature of disease and illness as it is conceived by the natives, their own methods and criteria for classifying disease, the causes and cures, types of therapists and healers, their skills and socio-medical roles, preventive measures between medicine and religion and the cultural and symbolic aspects of medicine (Hughes, 1968); Foster G. M. (1978); Tribhuwan Robin (1998); Turner Victor (1967); Lieban Richard (1973); Mun Nancy (1973); Cameroff Jean (1981); Murray David (1977) etc.

(c) Some of the Areas of Ethno-Medicine are:

1. Illness ideology.
2. Body image and symbolism.
3. Ritual healing.
4. Nature and role of ethno-medical specialists including herbalists, bone setters, shamans and midwives.
5. Ethno-medical therapies including herbal or chemo therapy, mechanical and magico-religious therapy.
6. Mother and child health.
7. Preventive, promotive and curative medicine.
8. Impact of cultural symbols on the psyche of patients etc.

In his paper on the "scope of ethno-medical science", Fabrega (1977) has stated that ethno-medicine deals with information pertaining to social adaptation, deviant behaviour, illness, disease, medical taxonomy, folk medical knowledge and system of care. Some of the problems inherent in studying these issues include:

(a) What is illness and what is not?
(b) The role of a sick person.
(c) The interpretation of systems.
(d) Treatment of illness.
(e) Institutions used for treatment.
(f) Organisation and quality of medical systems.

Well, it is evident from the above theoretical frame work, that people everywhere act on the basis of knowledge and beliefs, about the world, about themselves. That health is an aspect of culture and hence beliefs and practices regarding health and disease are culturally governed.

The medical interpretation of health, disease, body image, nature and role of medical doctors, the therapies, surgeries, medicines administered, rehabilitation and hospitalization is totally different from people's (insider's) perception.

Musculo-skeletal disorders and problems are no exception to this rule. This book has made an humble beginning to educate the readers, policy makers, doctors and orthopaedic surgeons, that rural and tribal people have different beliefs, ideas and knowledge about bones, sprains, strains, skeletal system, fractures, body image etc.

This book has been written keeping in view the different castes, ethnic groups, nomadic communities and tribes, that from 65-70 per cent of India's rural population. They have their own socio-cultural perceptions regarding musculo-skeletal disorders and problems.

HYPOTHESIS

Based on the review of literature, pilot studies and primary data gathered, the authors have developed following hypothesis.

1. That , people's perceptions of origin and cause of certain musculo-skeletal disorders are influenced by cultural beliefs.
2. People co-relate the causes of injuries, fractures, swellings, bone tumors, sprain, pain, backache and other musculo-skeletal disorders to bad luck, sins in past birth, breach

of cultural taboos, wrath of gods & goddesses, wrong combination of food, accident, evil eye, imbalance & disturbance of blood flow, impact of hot & cold environment, occupational hazards and life styles.

3. Ethno-nutritional beliefs and practices of people are an aspect of their culture.
4. Socio-economic and educational status of patients suffering from musculo-skeletal disorders is directly proportional to the expenditure incurred in orthopaediatric treatment received by them.
5. The tendency of shifting therapy, to get fast cure and relief from pain is common among patients suffering musculo-skeletal disorders.
6. That, patients with physical disability and amputation suffer from psychological trauma, inferiority complex and social stigma.
7. That, the response of a family & society towards care and rehabilitation of patients with musculo – disorder varies.

OBJECTIVES OF THE STUDY

Keeping in view the theoretical framework, hypothesis and primary data, the objectives of the study are:

1. To explore people's perceptions of body image, skeletal system, bones, muscles, fractures, strains, sprains etc.
2. To study ethno-nutritional beliefs and practices with reference to growth of bones, skeletal system and muscles in particular.
3. To understand people's ideology with reference etiology of selected musculo-skeletal disorders and problems.
4. To understand the response of family and society to musculo-skeletal disorders, physical disability and injuries.
5. To unveil the perceptions, views attitudes and problems of people that revolve around the economics of orthopaedic treatment.
6. To unravel the co-relation between people's habits, life styles, occupations, class, work culture, working conditions and low backache.

7. To study the perceptions of Gonds and Thakur's about osteoporosis.
8. To explore the socio-cultural perceptions of sickle cell patients with physical disability regarding the skeletal manifestations and bone changes.
9. To study the nature and role of traditional bone setters and analyze the gaps of scientific orthopaedic knowledge, diagnosis, practice and treatment given by them to the rural and tribal folks.
10. To suggest further areas of research.

2

Research Methodology

INTRODUCTION

Social science research basically aims to explore, why people behave the way they do ? Human beings are the most complex social animals on the face of this planet, because there is cultural variation in the way they behave. What is considered to be a deviance in one society, may not be the same in the other society. The methods of investigation in social sciences are different than those of the pure sciences.

Studying a medical phenomena from an anthropological or sociological perspective is not an easy task. However, the present study, which basically focuses on understanding the socio-cultural dimensions of selected musculo-skeletal disorders was a combined attempt of an Anthropologist as well as an Orthopaedic surgeon, who worked together for a period of 3½ years in General Hospital's Orthopedic Department of Gadchiroli district, in the state of Maharashtra, India.

The book contains Thirteen Chapters, out of which nine chapters are based on primary data collected from the respondents not only in Gadchiroli, but other parts of Maharashtra. The authors have provided methodological details in every data chapter, presented in the book.

Use of secondary data, citations of Orthopaedic experts, social scientists and medical doctors has been quoted in relevant portions of the book. The primary data chapters is both quantitative and qualitative in nature. The quantitative and qualitative data presented has been analyzed using excel, software as well manual techniques.

The authors did conduct pilot studies, before actually understanding a given musculo-skeletal disorder, Efforts have been made to conduct cross-cultural studies.

TARGET POPULATION

A Comparative analysis of different tribal, caste and non-tribal groups has been presented in the book. Every data chapter makes a note of the target population studied.

PRIMARY AND SECONDARY SOURCES OF DATA

Both primary and secondary data has been gathered to study the various musculo-skeletal disorders and the socio-cultural dimensions associated with the same.

RESEARCH TOOLS

Most basic tools of research in social sciences such as interview guide, interview schedule, Observation, case study method, photography etc. have used by the authors. Informal interviews and focused group discussions were carried out, where ever necessary.

ANALYSIS

As mentioned earlier, both quantitative and qualitative data was analyzed, following scientific methods.

CHAPTER SCHEME

The data has been presented in twelve different chapters in this book.

3

Etiology of Musculo-skeletal Disorders *Illness Episodes*

DISEASE, ILLNESS, HEALTH AND ETIOLOGY: CONCEPTS AND DEFINITIONS

Disease has been one of the fundamental problems faced by every human society and every known society has developed certain ways and means to cope up with disease, thereby creating a system of medicine. (Tribhuwan Robin & Gambhir R.D. 1995)

Anthropological interest in medicine stems from the fact that although health and disease are biological and medical phenomena they are deeply rooted in people's belief systems. It is to such beliefs and practices regarding health and disease which are products of indigenous culture and not merely derived from the conceptual framework of modern medicine, is referred to as ethno-medicine. (Hughes Charles, 1968)

The Oxford dictionary defines medicine, as an art of healing. The concept and practice of medicine is however viewed differently by allopath and traditional medical practitioners. In fact, medical science has always focused its attention to the study of causative factors in disease and illness and its domain has largely been in biological and physical science in dealing with problems of health and disease. They do not look beyond the bacillus or virus.

1. **What is Health ?**

The World Health Organisation (1948) has therefore defined health as a state of physical, mental, social and spiritual well being and not merely absence of disease.

The above definition certainly gives importance to socio-cultural, psychological and even spiritual aspects associated with human health. Concept of health, disease, disease classification and etiology varies from one culture to another.

Allan Young, an eminent Anthropologist has defined disease and illness as follows:

2. **Disease:** According to Allan Young disease is a mal-functioning of biological and psychological processes and systems of human beings.

Man is unique in having cultural environment. This includes all the conditions in which human beings are born, live, work, procreate and die. Culture as an environment is deeply related with the health of human beings.

Human cultures everywhere include patterns of social organisation, designed to regulate a particular society, the members can understand behaviour of most people and they can predict how an individual will react in a given situation. Health is an aspect of culture and hence disease, illness, disease classification, health and health seeking behaviour is defined culturally. People, who are not aware of modern medicine, scientific and biological constitution of human body, its anatomy physiology etc., follow culturally defined beliefs and practices regarding health and disease.

3. **Illness:** Illness is mal-functioning of psycho-social processes. Meaning, a person's disease is associated with interference of social, spiritual, cosmic, ancestral, evil etc causative agents and forces.

For example, "Nazar Lagana" (evil eye) is associated with an external social causative agent, who casts evil eye on a person, as a result of which he or she becomes ill. The concerned community members destroy the evil effect by conducting culturally acceptable healing rituals to ward off the evil effect. In North India, the ritual of warding off evil eye is known as, "Nazar Utarna".

Amputation of hand or leg is associated by patients in India to sins in past birth, karma (deeds), punishment by deities, wrath of gods and goddesses etc.

4. **Health:** In his book captioned, "Medical World of Tribals", Tribhuwan Robin (1998), has defined ill-health as a disharmony between body, mind, soul and society. It occurs due to the disruption of man's relationship with his fellowmen, other social groups, deities, evil spirits, ancestral spirits, cosmic forces and beings.
5. **Disease Classification:** People's perception of disease, its origin, cause and its classification differs, from that of the medical interpretation. For example, in North India Diarrhea is classified by people on the basis of the "colour" of the stool, namely "pila dasta" (yellow coloured stool diarrhea), "lal dasta" (red coloured stool diarrhea) and "hara dasta" (green coloured stool diarrhoea).

The Thakur Scheduled Tribe of Raigad District in Maharashtra classifies and differentiates Small Pox and Chicken pox on the basis of size of the boils on the body. They refer small pox to "Mothya Baya" (visitation of senior female planetary spirits), and chicken pox to "Lahan Baya" (visitation of junior female planetary spirits). It is pertinent to note at this juncture that small pox is eradicated, but "Mothya Baya" was the tern used for the disease. (Tribhuwan Robin, 1998)

6. **Culture, Environment and Disease**

As aptly pointed out by Hassan K.A (1979), the study of the circumstances for development of specific disease in specific groups of people is included in epidemiology. With reference to any particular disease, the possible etiological factors have been divided into three main groups:

(a) **The Causative Agents:** The causative agents which include virus, bacterium, protozoa, parasitic worms and toxic chemicals.

(b) **The Environmental Factors:** The environmental factors responsible for favouring the development and spread of the disease can be broadly classified into two categories namely:

   (i) **Natural Factors** – these include soil, temperature, humidity, fauna and flora.

   (ii) **Socio-Cultural Factors** – these include social, mental, spiritual and material aspects of man.

(c) **The Host Factors:** This means that man acts as a host to various causative agents.

Infection or infestation has to be seen as an expression of the continuous and constant struggle of living beings for food by predation of parasitism, for shelter and for propagation of their kind. The importance of hereditary factors in this host – parasitic relationship is also to be recognized.

ILLNESS EPISODES

Given, the above background, let us look into people's perceptions of origin and cause to muscular – skeletal disorders. In this section of the chapter few illness episodes have been documented related to a few muscular – skeletal disorders. What is an illness episode?

An illness episode or therapeutic narrative is one to which Evelyn Early (1982: 1481) refers to as a commentary on illness progression, curative actions and surrounding events both relevant and irrelevant fragments embedded in the conversation, which are framed by stylistic shifts that are evidently codified into elaborate accounts and which are reference of years of experience after the illness episode.

Illness Episode No. 1

Residial Paralysis of the Arm

1. Aim of the Illness Episode

To unveil the beliefs and practices people associate with etiology and therapeutic practices with residial paralysis of the arm.

2. Background of the Case

Mrs. Madhuri Vasant Dumane, a married woman, aged 40, having three children is a house wife of an agriculture labourer. Madhuri is married, since the last 17 years. Her husband, on an average earns Rs. 20,000/- per annum. It is difficult for the family to meet ends. The family belongs to "Dhiwar" – a fishing folk caste group. At times they fish, to get some cash, in times of crisis.

3. Course of Events

Madhuri's arm is paralyzed since birth. She cannot lift the same as there is no sensation. Her parents were worried and spend about Rs. 5000/- on her treatment, but nothing worked. At the age of 23, she was married to an agriculture labourer. Her husband, Vasant, took lot of efforts to treat her paralyzed arm. He took her to a famous bone setter from Thane Gaon, Armori Tahsil, of Gadchiroli District. The bone setter charged her Rs. 2000/- for the treatment, but was not successful. He must have spend Rs. 15,000/- for her treatment, by going to traditional bone setters, herbalists and shamans, including orthopeadic surgeons.

Madhuri, being a dependent housewife, feels very strong that her husband had to spend so much money on her treatment. Finally she and her husband went to a shaman, who is a devotee of "Arjundev". The shaman instructed them to offer "Arjundev" a chicken sacrifice every year. The couple has been doing it since the last five years. The shaman interpreted the cause of her paralysis to wrath of gods and goddesses. Hence, they sacrifice, every year. The shaman applies ash on her arm after the sacrifice.

Analysis

What comes spiritually, must be healed spiritually, hence the couple opted to sacrifice a chicken to "Arjundev", every year. Both Madhuri and her husband are illiterate and poor. The illness of Madhuri has become a social issue for the family. The unsuccessful treatment of the disease and their futile efforts in seeking herbal, mechanical and other treatment has forced them to believe that the etiology of the illness is deeply rooted in intervention of supernatural pathogenic agents. The couple is unaware and ignored of the medical or scientific cause of paralysis of her arm.

Illness Episode No. 2

Amputed Leg and Social Stigma

1. Aim of the Illness Episode

To highlight the social stigma associated with amputation of leg of a young boy.

2. Background of the Case

Rajesh Laxman Burungwar, aged 16, a male, belonging to "Burud" (Basket Maker), left school while in the seventh grade. Rajesh has three sisters, who are married. He is the only son of his parents. His father is a daily wage labourer who earns Rs. 9600/- per annum. Rajesh left school and started working as a daily wage labourer, at the age of 15 years. He worked in a saw mill, owned by a Forest Department Contractor.

3. Course of Events

On the 7th of June, 2012, when Rajesh went to work at the saw mill, he was sitting on few logs of wood. Next to him some labourers were cutting wood with electric saw. Rajesh wanted to get down from the heap of logs. While getting down, he slipped and fell close to the electric saw. In the process he cut his right leg. He was rushed to the general hospital in Chandrapur. The orthopeadic surgeon had to amput his leg and performs a surgery.

4. Analysis

On 6/7/2012, Rajesh came to General Hospital, Gadchiroli, to get handicapped certificate. The researchers met him and interviewed him and his father. Rajesh's father, who is 60 years old, expressed his grief over the son's amputed leg. The father stated that Rajesh is my only son. After my death, he will carry our lineage name. The responsibility of feeding me and my wife lies on Rajesh. He must get married and procreate to carry on our family lineage. I am eagerly waiting to see my grand children, play with me, and tell them stories. He paused for a moment and exclaimed. This will only happen when Rajesh gets married. Who will get married to my handicapped son?

His friends and the neighborhood has already started teasing him as a lame (Langda) person. He is branded and stigmatized as an handicapped for life long. Getting him married, finding a proper job for him is my priority said the father. The family has spent Rs. 70,000/- on Rajesh's treatment till date.

There are several young boys like Rajesh who become victims of unexpected accidents and become handicapped or physically disabled. They are then stigmatized as handicapped by the society and face the social stigma for life long.

Stiffness of the Joints: Medical and Socio-Cultural Interpretation

(a) Medical Interpretation

Stiffness is defined as loss of 75 per cent or more of the normal movement. Given below is the classification of various joints of the upper and lower limb.

(i) Joints of the Upper Limb

(a) Stiffness of one shoulder.
(b) Stiffness of one elbow.
(c) Stiffness of one wrist.
(d) Stiffness of both shoulders.
(e) Stiffness of both elbows.
(f) Stiffness of both wrists.
(g) Stiffness of all fingers.
(h) Stiffness of all fingers in both the hands.

(ii) Joints of the Lower Limb

(a) Stiffness of one hip joint.
(b) Stiffness of one knee joint.
(c) Stiffness of one ankle joint.
(d) Stiffness of both the hip joints.

(e) Stiffness of both the knee joints.

(f) Stiffness of both the ankle joints.

(b) Stiffness of Upper and Lower Limb Joints: Socio-Cultural Interpretation

Contrary to the medical interpretation of stiffness of upper and lower limb joints, people everywhere have their own socio-cultural interpretation of stiffness. Given below is an illness episode that reveals people's perception of stiffness of bones.

Illness Episode No. 3

1. Aim of the Illness Episode

To unravel, the concept of stiffness of bones, among the Mavchis of Nandurbar.

2. Background of the Case

Mavchi is one of the Scheduled Tribes of north-western Maharashtra. This episode presents the perception of Mavchis regarding stiffness of bodily bones. Mr. ZX, aged 52, a male, married member of Mavchi tribe, of Navapur block, in Nandurbar district, Maharashtra state, narrates his episode as below.

3. Course of Events

Mr. ZX suffered from stiffness of bones of his right arm and right ankle; he could not move his right arm and right ankle fully. He visited two bone setters, who massaged his right arm and ankle with coconut oil and pongamia pinnatta oil, but this did not have any effect on Mr. ZX. He tried allopathic treatment in Navapur but failed to recover.

On enquiring the origin and cause of the stiffness, Mr. ZX revealed that stiffness of the bones of his right hand and right ankle occurred due to two factors namely:

(i) The nerves of his brains dried.

(ii) The water content and blood in his body became less.

4. Analysis

Mavchis co-relate stiffness of bones to drying up of brain nerves and reduction of water content and blood in the body.

Illness Episode No. 4

1. Aim of the Episode

To study, the concept of stiffness of fingers as viewed by a Thakur tribe.

2. Background of the Case

Walku, aged 50, a married male member of the Thakur tribe, a shaman, hails from Nagewadi, Pathraj village of Karjat block in Raigad district, in the state of Maharashtra. He was interviewed to understand his perception of one of his patients who was suffering from stiffness of finger of his left hand.

3. Shaman's Perception

Walku, a shaman by profession stated that the content of air, water, heat and blood in his patient's finger is absent and hence there is stiffness.

4. Analysis

Walku shaman's perception regarding stiffness of fingers revolves around his concept of less or no supply of air, heat, water and blood to the fingers, resulting into dry condition. He stated that bones which do not get supply of air, water, blood and heat dry up like dry sticks of a tree and become stiff. Walku co-related skeletal system of human beings to the trunk and branches of a tree.

Illness Episode No. 5

1. Aim of the Episode

To explore the perception of a Gond tribal woman regarding the origin and cause of paralysis.

2. Background of the Case

Mrs. MN, a Gond widow, lived with her son, who is a government employee in Aheri block of Gadchiroli district. She lived in a joint family. During the summer of 2007 Mrs. MN started sleeping near a air cooler, as it was hot.

3. Course of Events

Although she did not like to sleep near the cooler, she had to for the sake of her son, his wife and children, who could not sleep without the cooler. In fact one finds it very difficult to sleep or even work without cooler in summer. Mrs. MN's body was exposed to the cool air in the humid and hot atmosphere for 2 to 3 months. One fine morning she got paralysis attack. She was hospitalized. Her son did not take her to the local herbalists and masseurs.

4. Analysis

Mrs. MN, associated the origin and cause of her paralysis to constant exposure to cool sir while sleeping and of course during the day time.

Illness Episode No. 6

1. Aim of the Episode

To explore the perceptions of a Pardhan tribal about the origin and cause of paralysis.

2. Background of the Case

Namdev Kashinath Atram, a male member of Pardhan tribe, aged 72, married with fear children, a farmer, hails from Jewora village of Korpana block in Chandrapur district was interviewed to understand his concept regarding the etiology of paralysis.

3. Etiology of Paralysis

According Namdev mostly elderly people become victims of Paralysis, because their bones are weak, there is less blood in their body which is not thick. The colour of their blood is blackish red. The flow and circulation of the blood is slow and abnormal. They become victims of paralysis because blood becomes less in one part of the body, right from head till toe. Blood circulation in the affected part becomes abnormal. There is no strength in that part of the body and hence the victim becomes paralyzed.

4. Analysis

Namdev's perception regarding the origin and cause of paralysis revolves around his concept of blackish red blood, less blood supply and abnormal blood circulation, resulting into weak muscles, bones and lack of strength. These multiple factors cause paralysis.

Illness Episode No. 7

1. Aim of the Episode

To study the origin and cause of paralysis, as viewed by the non-tribals in Nagar district.

2. Background of the Case

The researchers conducted informal discussions with seven non-tribal groups in seven villages of Ahmednagar district on different occasions to understand the perceptions of non-tribal groups mostly belonging to various castes in rural areas of the district, regarding paralysis.

3. Perception

One of the standard response that came in these informal discussions was cold air passes over one part of the body of a victim, makes it numb completely and hence the person becomes paralyzed. The popular term for this etiological concept is "Eka Anga Varun Varâ Jane", meaning air passing over one side or half a part of the body.

4. Analysis

This concept reminds a researcher that people believe that cold air passes over half part of a person's body, making it numb and strength less, thereby resulting into paralysis.

Illness Episode No. 8

1. Aim of the Episode

To understand how a Thakur tribal co-relates the fracture of ulna to breach of cultural taboo.

2. Background of the Case

Mr. B, a male aged 43, married with two children, a small scale cultivator, hails from Kharbachi Wadi, of Kikvi village, in Karjat block of Raigad district in Maharshtra. Every year, Mr. B offers a hen to Waghdev (tiger god), before sowing rice. During the year 1991, he failed to do so.

That, harvesting season, he got fewer yields as compared to 1990. More importantly, during the month of November, 1991, when Mr. B climbed a tree to fetch some fuel wood, he fell down and broke his fore arm ulna bone. He approached a bone setter, who did set the bone using conventional method, but pain would not stop.

Mr. B then approached a shaman (Bhagat), who ritually diagnosed the origin and cause of his illness and told him that his pain and the fracture was the result of breach of cultural taboo and wrath of tiger god.

4. Analysis

Mr. B co-related the origin and cause of his fracture and pain to breach of cultural taboo and wrath of Waghdev (the tiger god).

Illness Episode No. 9

1. Aim of the Episode

To study the origin and cause of bone tumor, as perceived by a rural elderly man.

2. Background of the Case

G7, an elderly man aged 56 from Jeevti village, in Chandrapur was admitted in Gadchiroli general hospital. He had a round lump on his left knee. The doctors asked him to take an x-ray. G7 was diagnosed for a bone tumor. The orthopeadic surgeon operated him and removed the tumor.

3. Course of Events

G7 had this problem since he was 48 years old. He said the size of the lump was increasing over the years. He showed it to the doctors in Gadchiroli, when he was in pain. His family members tried several herbal therapies and massage techniques thinking, the lump will reduce in size. Finally, he landed in the hospital and had to undergo surgery.

When the doctors told him about the tumor, his relatives were shocked. His mother said that the tumor was a result of witchcraft. Their neighbors were jealous of the progress of G7 and his family. The mother of G7 believed that their neighbors have ritually inserted a charmed "Lime" into the knee of G7.

4. Analysis

In the instant case the mother of the patient believed that her son's bone tumor was a result of witchcraft.

Illness Episode No. 10

1. Aim of the Episode

To study the cause of multiple fractures, as perceived by a rural inhabitants.

2. Background of the Case

B10, a male aged 38, a member of Mali (Gardener) caste, hails from Savali village, of Chandrapur district, was amputed because he met with an accident. His right leg had multiple fractures on both tibia and fibula bones. He was banged by a Jeep, while crossing the road on his bike.

3. Analysis

B10 was injured very badly after the accident that the doctors had no option but to am put his right foot from below the knee. The young man was shocked and suffered with pain. His pain and agony made him believe that he must have committed sins in past birth.

Illness Episode No. 11

1. Aim of the Episode

To unveil the perception of the Mavchis regarding sprains, their causes and therapy.

2. Background of the Case

Jatyra, aged 23, a married member of the Bhil tribe, from Navapur block of Nandurbar district in the state of Maharashtra. His ankle had a severe sprain and swelling as a stone fell on it, while working at the road construction site for the Public Works Department.

3. Course of Events

Jatrya was hurt at 11 am in the morning and soon realized that ankle and feet turned greenish-blue in colour. He had pain. His brother took him home on a bicycle. Jatrya's wife heated some water and slowly massaged the swelling with a cloth soaked in hot water. That, evening Jatrya's brother got some Palash leaves (Beautia Monosporma) heated them and tied around the swelling. The leaves were tied for two days.

The procedure of heating leaves and tying on the ankle was repeated 2 to 3 times. The swelling was reduced after a week.

4. Analysis

The Mavchi's believe that sprains and swellings are caused if any part of human body is banged against a hard surface, or hit by a stone or crushed. Depending on the severity of the bang, knock or crush, it turns blue-black. They say that the muscles are hurt. Palash leaves have the healing capacity to erase the blue-black colour and reduce the swelling as well.

Illness Episode No. 12

1. Aim of the Episode

To study the perceptions of the Warli tribe's regard the causes of low backache.

2. Background of the Case

The researchers conducted a Focused Group Interview of 32 Warli men and women, in Rajadpada of Raitali village, in Dahanu block of Thane district, to unveil their perceptions regarding the origin and cause of low backache.

3. Analysis

Some of the responses that emerged through the Focused Group Discussion regarding causes of low backache were as below:

(i) Continuous bending while performing agriculture work such as sowing, weeding, transplanting, harvesting and threshing.

(ii) Lifting heavy weight.

(iii) Improper sleeping habits.

(iv) Fall on the back.

(v) Walking long distances with heavy loads of fire wood, timber, grain bags etc on the head.

(vi) Sorcery, witchcraft and black magic etc.

Focused Group Discussions contribute in giving information commonly shared by a group or a society. In the instant case an overview of the low backache etiology was documented by the researchers as viewed by the Warli's from an insider's perspective.

Illness Episode No. 13

1. Aim of the Episode

To explore the perceptions of low backache, as viewed by the coolies.

2. Background of the Case

The researchers carried out yet another Focused Group Discussion with 15 coolies from Market Yard area of Pune city, to unveil their perceptions regarding the origin and cause of low backache.

3. Analysis

The discussion held with the coolies, who carry food grain bags that weigh 100 kgs, daily for several years revealed that the pressure of the weight of the bag, the improper walking posture, age factor, vigor and continuous taxing on the back bones causes low backache among the coolies.

An analysis of the above given illness episodes of patients suffering from musculo-skeletal disorder reveals that disease etiology is culturally determined and interpreted. That people everywhere have beliefs regarding the origin and cause of illness. That, there are natural, spiritual, cosmic, ancestral, religious pathogenic agents that cause musculo-skeletal disorders and problems. That, what comes spiritually has to be healed spiritually hence the role of shamans, religious ritual healing etc comes into play. That, the level of awareness regarding the scientific origin and cause of musculo-skeletal disorders is less or absent among the tribal and rural masses in India.

Illness Episode No. 14

1. Aim of the Episode

To unveil the etiology of Osteocondroma – a tumour that arises from the bone.

2. Background

Mukesh Dadaji Chaudhari, aged 20 years, a bachelor, belonging to the Kunbi caste, hails from Savarkheda village of Kurkheda block of Gadchiroli district, in the state of

Maharashtra, India. Mukesh suffered from Osteocondroma, a tumor that arises from a bone.

He was admitted in Gadchiroli general hospital on 6th of November, 2012, for operating the tumour on the right femur above the knee. He said he had not consulted a traditional bone setter nor a Shaman.

3. Course of Events

Dadaji suffered from this disease since he was five years old. The size of the tumour then was small. However, as he was nearing the age of marriage, both Dadaji and his parents started worrying. The family members wanted to operate the tumor, when Dadaji was 15 years of age. Somehow it did not work then.

Dadaji said the local name of this disease (Osteocondroma) is "bend" – meaning a mass of flesh or bone. On enquiring why he took the decision of surgery, Dadaji stated that he was to get married soon and that he did not want his to be wife to see the tumor. On enquiring, the cause for the tumor, Dadaji said, it was hereditary. Some members of his paternal side had the problem and hence he felt it was hereditary.

4. Analysis

Dadaji being from a upper caste, educated up to XIIth grade and exposed to urban and modern life, he did not go the traditional bone setter or the Shaman. He opted to get operated instead. He was however, unaware of the scientific name and cause of the disease. He called the disease as "bend" – which means a round mass of flesh or bone. That, according to Dadaji, the disease was caused, because it was in his family.

Illness Episode No. 15

1. Aim of the Episode

To unravel the cause of clavicle bone fracture, perceived by the Gonds.

2. Background

Mr. MG, aged 45, a male member of the Gond tribe, hails from Nandadi village, of Korchi block, Gadchiroli District in

Maharashtra state, India. He was admitted in general hospital in Gadchiroli.

3. Course of Events

Mr. MG was in a bullock cart, sitting near the driver on the edge of the cart. While the cart was in motion, he fell from the cart and the wheel went over his clavicle and it broke in the process. His x-ray was taken on 4th November, 2012 and was to be operated. However, the orthopaedic surgeon, refused to operate the patient as the surgery was complicated clavicle surgery was complicated. Clavicle surgery is rarely done by the orthopaedic surgeons; as such fractures occur rarely and needs experience to do so.

4. Analysis

In rural areas falls from a bullock cart are common. People often fall and break their bones. In the instant case the patient fell and the wheel of the cart went over clavicle bone. If the bone is not fixed the patient lives with it lifelong.

Etiology of Musculo-Skeletal Disorders

The illness episodes narrated in chapter three reveal that people associate the origin and cause of some musculo-skeletal disorders to:

1. Breach of cultural taboos.
2. Sins in past birth.
3. Influence of cold air on the body.
4. Imbalance in blood and water content in the body.
5. Drying up of nerves and reduction of blood in the body.
6. Accidents and falls.
7. Heredity.
8. Wrath of gods and goddesses.
9. Black magic and witchcraft.
10. Bad luck or misfortune.

THE PATIENT: A PERSON WITH ILLNESS

In his edited book captioned patients, physicians and illness, by Jaco G.E. (1958:246) has revealed how an individual who becomes sick is confronted with entirely new set of expectations and assumes entirely different patterns of behaviour, in carrying out the role of the patient. His illness, his reactions, to the experience of pain, to the physician and his ministrations, and to the others comprising the patient's milieu.

Further, Henry Lederer (1958:247) analyzes the orientation of the sick person as he views his surroundings in the hospital during the process of medical treatment. He states that the experience of illness is a complex psychological situation.

Pointing out the various stages of illness experience, Lederer stated that there are three stages namely:

(i) The transition from health to illness;
(ii) The period of accepted illness and;
(iii) Convalescence.

Upon falling ill most persons become aware of undesirable, unpleasant, and painful sensations of a disturbing reduction in strength and stamina; of a diminution in ability to perform habitual acts. For example; on the onset of fractures, sprains, strains and injuries a patient experiences pain, agony and unpleasant sensations.

When a patient has accepted diagnostic and initial therapeutic procedures, he enters another district time period in his experience of illness. Speaking of how the sick view their world Lederer (1958) states that a patient behaves differently when he is sick. His actions, thoughts and feelings are regressive in response to the child like world of illness. The main features of this behaviour are:

(i) Egocentric;
(ii) Construction of interests;
(iii) Emotional dependency;
(iv) Hypochondriasis

During the stage of illness, like a child the patient is concerned with matters of satisfying himself with needs for food, rest, absence of pain, physical comfort and relief of bodily tensions such as the urge to urinate, defecate, pass flatus or belch. The patient often presumes that his attendants share in these pre-occupations and he feels resentful or hurt if the doctor or nurse is distracted by other concerns.

Lastly, convalescence is the time period of transition from illness back into a state of health. This recovery of health involves a return of physical strength and a re-integration of the personality of the patient who has been living, feeling and thinking inregresseds, more or less infantile way.

The success of helping the patient, in the instant case suffering from musculo-skeletal disorders and problems depends on his "adolescent", social and emotional status, which then should call forth from his medical attendant's attitudes similar to those of the parents who encourage and aid the growth of adolescent children. Medical and paramedical staff should create opportunities for re-establishing self-confidence through success.

It is pertinent to note that the religious faith of the patient can quite feasibly influence his attitude towards medical treatment. In their paper captioned, "Ethno-Medical Pathway: A Conceptual Model", Tribhuwan Robin and Gambhir R.D. (1955) have demonstrated the various phases and shift in medical therapies that a tribal passes, while seeking treatment.

There is a need to study the phases of illness of patients suffering from various musculo-skeletal disorders in both government and private hospital settings. The attitudes of orthopaedic patients towards the efficacy of different systems in medical systems such as Ayurveda, Unani, Homoepathy, Naturopathy etc needs to be documented. Further, the shifts in changing therapies by the patients also needs to be documented.

4

The Economics of Musculo-skeletal Therapy

The good physician knows his patients through and through, and his knowledge is brought dearly. Time, sympathy and understanding must be lavishly dispensed, but the reward is to be found in that personal bond which forms the greatest satisfaction of the practice of medicine. One of the essential qualities of the clinician is interest in humanity, for the secret of the case of patients is in caring for the patient.

Dr. Francis Weld Peabody
Lecturer to Harvard Medical Students, 1927

THE ECONOMICS OF HEALTH EXPENDITURE

Technological advancement, impact of written and digital media, formal education, modernization, health education and awareness programmes, urbanization, planned development programmes, globalization and efforts of non-governmental organisations have certainly contributed in creating awareness of preventive, promotive and curative health among people. The rapid establishment of fitness, yoga, walking and laughing clubs in the cities is a proof of the increasing health consciousness among people.

People therefore spend money on purchasing good food, vegetables, cereals, fruits, nuts, dry fruits, mineral water, morning walks, exercises, visits to swimming pools, fitness clubs, yoga classes, seminars on healthy living and diet etc have become part and parcel of peoples life world over.

This chapter throws light on the economics of health expenditure with reference to musculo-skeletal disorders and its treatment. An attempt has been made to present a debate over how people's social, educational and economic status is directly proportional to health expenditure, be it preventive, promotive and curative with reference to musculo-skeletal disorders and their treatment.

Medical doctors have written extensively about health economics. Given below is the definition of the concept and the different types of health economic analysis.

What is health economics?

Mc Guire A and others (1988) have defined health economics as the study of the financial aspects of a healthcare system. In health economics, the goal is to put a monetary value on goods and services provided by healthcare professionals and the result of these goods and services on the patients they are treating.

Thakker Neil C.J. (2010:128) states that all health care systems have limited financial resources, thus it is very important to use these resources as efficiently as possible. This is true in both public healthcare systems in which healthcare is subsidized by the government and private healthcare systems where healthcare is usually funded by health insurance. (Creese A & Parker D, 1994)

Bhandari Mohit and Sancheti Parag (2010:119-122) have provided four types of economic analysis namely:

1. **Cost minimization analysis:** Here the underlying assumption is that treatments being compared have exactly equal out comes. Costs are compared to determine which treatment is more efficient and hence is the simplest form of economic analysis. (Schulman K., Seils D., 2010:129)

2. **Cost effective analysis:** Effective cost analysis is determined by quantitative measures. Examples include the number of hospitalization prevented, the number of years of life gained, the number of successful treatments and the time to relapse.
3. **Cost utility analysis:** Can be thought as a variation of cost-effectiveness analysis, since the only difference is that now, effectiveness is adjusted to reflect the relative value individuals place on it. (Ibid, 2010)
4. **Cost-benefit analysis:** It is essentially a variation of cost-effectiveness analysis.

Case Study No. 1
I Prefer to Bear the Pain and Die: Says a Patient with Hip fracture

Mr. K, a male, aged 52, a member of a scheduled caste community, a labourer from Saoli block of Gadchiroli, fell down from a tree, while plucking tendu leaves. He broke his hip bone and was advised surgery, by a private orthopaedic doctor in Gadchiroli.

The approximate expense for the surgery, medicines, implants, physiotherapy and hospitalization as revealed by the private orthopaedic surgeon was Rs. 70,000. He was advised to go to the general hospital run by the government in Chandrapur. The health staff stated that, the surgery and treatment is free, but you will have to spend money on implants, medicines, transportation etc which works out to be Rs. 30,000.

Mr. K, who is a labourer, hardly earning a cash of Rs. 7-8 thousand per annum, is landless with a rented house, is socio-economically backward, said, that I prefer bear the pain and die, because I cannot afford to pay that much amount.

The analysis of the above case study simply reveals that economic inability to bear the expense of a orthopaedic disorder such as hip fracture and surgery super-sides or over rides a poor patients pain, agony and misery. He gives priority to live with pain till death, rather than treating the same.

India has several patients like Mr. K, who need the attention of health service providers and policy makers.

Case Study No. 2

We were Unaware of the Tumor on the Femur Bone: Ignorant Parents

Mr. C, aged 16, a male, belonging to Madgi caste, hails from Saoli, block in Gadchiroli district, fell while playing in the school, and broke his left femur bone. He was admitted in the orthopaedics ward of general hospital in Gadchiroli.

The patient was sent for x-ray, by the senior orthopaedic surgeon. On examining the x-ray it was found that there was a tumor on the lower part of the left femur bone. The x-ray was shown to the parents. Their consent for operating the lad was taken. On 6/9/2012, the boy was operated, the tumor was removed and the bone was fixed, using implants.

The family spent Rs. 10,000 on the implants medicine, hospitalization including transport. They could afford to pay the amount, as the father of the patient borrowed money from a money lender with five percent interest.

The moral of the case study, reveals, that there are patients who take treatment in government hospitals, pay for implants, medicines, hospitalization and transportation by borrowing money on interest.

Case Study No. 3

I Sold my Agriculture Land for Amputation

Mr. N, a married male aged 55, a member of Mali (Gardener) caste, studied up to grade 3, a small scale cultivator had a crooked ankle since he was 42 years old. He was walking with a limp, till he was operated twice by a private orthopaedic surgeon from Chandrapur. The ankle became crooked as a result of a fracture, which was ignored by him.

After the operation Mr. N, walked with the help of crèches. He spend Rs. One Lakh on his surgeries. He sold his one acre agriculture land for 80,000/-. Despite of all this, his ankle remained crooked. On 23/01/2012, he was admitted in

General Hospital, Gadchiroli. He requested the orthopaedic surgeon to amput his ankle. However, his ankle was amputed, due to legal reasons.

The result of the episode was that:

1. Despite of two operations and spending Rs. One Lakh, his surgery was not successful.
2. He lost his only acre agriculture land.
3. He felt guilty that he snatched his only son's bread and butter by selling the land.
4. He had to live in pain and agony for rest of his life.
5. Psychologically he was distributed because, he would be dependent on his son and wife, for rest of his life.
6. He could not afford to buy good quality crutches. A carpenter in his village made crutches worth Rs. 100/-.

Case Study No. 4

Thank God, I had Money in my General Provident Fund

Mr. M, a married male, aged 56, a member of the Gond Scheduled Tribe, a stenographer by profession, has four daughters, works in the Tribal Development Department, Government of Maharashtra. He fell while riding his mobike, and broke his right femur bone. He was taken to an orthopaedic surgeon in Chandrapur. The doctor advised surgery and insertion of a rod.

Mr. M spend Rs. 18,000/- on the surgery in the year 2004. A year later, he discovered that there was infection in the operated area. He approached the same private orthopaedic surgeon, who recommended second surgery, Mr. M, had to pay Rs. 25,000/- the second time. His rod was removed and was given antibiotics for healing. The surgery was however successful. Mr. M, landed up paying nearly Rs. 50,000/- on both the surgeries, including medicine and hospitalization.

Although, Mr. M is a government servant, and has four daughters and his wife who are dependent on him. He would have found it extremely difficult to pay for the surgery, had he not had money in the General Provident Fund. There are several single earners in government sector who are saved from major expenses because of General Provident Fund.

Case Study No. 5

We Spend 3 Lakhs on our Daughter's Surgery

Mrs. P is a teacher in a Convent School in Pune. Her husband is a Government Servant. They have an apartment of their own. In the year 1998 a daughter was born in the family. The baby girl grew up well, when she was 4½ years of age her parents observed that the girl slightly limped. They approached the best orthopaedic surgeon in Pune city.

An x-ray of her hip was taken and it was found out that the girl had congenital dislocation of the hip. The head of the femur of her left leg was not in the socket. The parents decided to operate her. They spent Rs. 30,000/- on their five year old daughter, who had 20 stitches. She was hospitalized for 20 days. Her cast was removed; she had boils and rash on her hip region. Parents spend another Rs. 10,000/- on her physiotherapy treatment. To their surprise, the so called eminent orthopaedic surgeon had not put the bone in the socket and wanted to do two more surgeries on the innocent child.

The parents lost trust and faith in Indian orthopaedic surgeons and took their daughter to the USA for second surgery. The orthopaedic surgeon operated the girl successfully. Even to remove the clips. The father of the girl accompanied the daughter to the USA second time. The operation was successful. The moral of the case was the ignorant educated parents spent 3 lakhs on her treatment. The orthopaedic surgeon in USA spend another 10,000 US dollars on her surgery hospitalization and physiotherapy.

Case Study No. 6

Rich Sports Persons go Abroad for Orthopaedic Surgery and Treatment

A budding cricketer from Pune had an individual fracture of the left fore-arm, as he fell down while fielding a cricket ball, during his net practice. He was interviewed by the authors to explore how much he spent on the treatment. He stated that he spend Rs. 20,000/- on the same.

On interviewing him, on the role of sports organisations in spending money on their treatment. He said, I am a small sports person, and can't afford to go to the best surgeon and physiotherapist. However, rich and popular cricketers and sports persons go abroad to the best hospitals, orthopaedic surgeons and physiotherapists for treatment, he said.

Case Study No. 7

Economically well-off People Seek Best of the Best Orthopaedic Treatment

Mr. D, an eminent business man aged 43, hails from an economically well-off family, slipped in his bathroom, while having a shower. He broke his forearm. His family members immediately rushed him to a best hospital in Bombay. The family members of the patient met the hospital manager and instructed him to get the best of the best orthopaedic expert to attend to Mr. D.

He was kept in a posh and single special room in the hospital with best of the best facilities. The analysis of the instant case reveals that there are very rich people in India, who can afford best of the best quality treatment for orthopaedic disorders.

Case Study No. 8

The Traditional Bone Setter Charged only Rs. 200/-

Mrs. TN, aged 50, a married female, belonging to Madgi caste, hails from a village near Armori block of Gadchiroli district. She slipped and fell on her right side and took the support of her fingers of the right hand. Her middle and index finger broke. She had swelling on both the fingers. Her son took her to a traditional bone setter residing in Thane Gaon, about five kilometers away from their village.

On reaching Thane Gaon, the bone setter checked the fracture using palpation method, diverted the attention of the patient by talking to her and within a fraction of a second he pulled her index finger and set the bone. He repeated the same technique to fix her middle finger bone. He then applied medicated (Jawas) oil, put cotton layer on both the fingers and tied them tightly with crape bandage separately.

The patient was asked not to remove the bandage for 15 days. She was given a sling to hold her hand in an horizontal posture. He also gave her herbal powder to consume twice a day with milk. He charged her Rs. 200/- for the treatment. The woman patient could not afford treatment even in a government hospital and hence landed up in the bone setters zone. One gets to see several such patients who visit bone setters.

Case Study No. 9

We gave 5 kilogram (Dhan) Rice with Husk to the Tribal bone setter

Miss TX, aged 15, a female member of Madia tribe, hails from Laheri village of Bhamragad block in Gadchiroli District. Miss. TX fell from a tree while plucking tendu leaves and broke her right ankle. Her father tied her ankle with a cloth and rushed her to a tribal bone setter in a nearby village.

The tribal bone setter diagnosed her, using palpation method and fixed her bone. He applied herbal medicine on her ankle and tied her ankle with cloth. He advised her to use crutches for a month. The father of the patient, gave 5 kilogram rice with husk to the bone setter, for his services.

In most interior and remote tribal areas tribal bone setters, midwives, herbalists and shamans are given gifts in kind in the form of cereals, pulses, vegetables, liquor, coconut or clothes for the services they render.

Paying in kind and not in cash is a part and parcel of the cultural life of tribals who survive on collection of minor forest produce, fishing, hunting and small scale cultivation.

Case Study No. 10

I Spend Rs. 15,000/- on Ayurvedic (Kerala Style) Massage per month: A Businessman

Mr. A, aged 52, a married male is a cooperator in Pune Municipal Corporation is suffering from backache and arthritis of knee joints. Besides, being a politician he has construction business, auto spare part shops and agriculture land. Economically, he is well-off. He spends Rs. 15,000/- per month to have Ayurvedic Massage in a Kerala Ayurvedic Massage Centre, every month. Every week he gets himself massaged. Kerala Ayurvedic massage is a costly affair and can be afforded by only economically well-off people.

Case Study No. 11

A Local Masseur Charges Rs. 200/- for Massage per Sitting

Mr. KP, aged 49, a married male, with two kids is a principal of a social service college in Nagpur. Mr. KP gets himself massaged from a local masseur every Sunday. The masseur charges him Rs. 200/- per sitting.

Both Mr. KP and his wife are professors and fetch nearly Rs. 1, 50,000/- per month's salary. Since Mr. KP has come up from a poverty stricken background, he prefers to get massaged by spending Rs. 800/- per month. He does it to relax and get relief from administrative stress and tension. Also to keep his muscles and bones fit.

Case Study No. 12

We Set up a Mini-hospital for our Dad's Treatment

Mr. DS and SS are two sons of an industrialist in Bombay. Their father, who is 73 years old has osteoporosis, had a fall in the bathroom and broke his femur bone. He was admitted in the best of the best hospitals in Bombay.

The orthopaedic surgeons carried out a surgery and fixed the bone. The patient was however advised strict best rest and was to move on a wheel chair, until the fracture healed. Mr. DS and his brother SS, who lived in joint family in Walkeshwar, moved their father to their bungalow in Juhu.

The entire bungalow was converted into a mini-hospital. Both the sons hired services of an orthopaedic surgeon, a full time doctor, two nurses, two ward boys and a sweeper. They did have their own watchman as well. The hired staff was well paid. There was a maid servant specially to take their father around on the wheel chair.

Mr. DS and SS could pay lakhs of rupees for a period of 4-5 months till their father recovered fully, because they had enough money. In fact spending money in lakhs was not the issue. Making their father's stay in the bungalow comfortable was important.

There are rich people in India like Mr. DS and SS for whom money is no big deal. The comfort, peace and happiness of their family member is essential. They have so much money that they can create a mini hospital in their bungalows and flats.

Case Study No. 13

I can't Afford to Spend Time in the Hospital

Mr. S a famous actor, fractured his hand, during a shoot. He was admitted in the hospital for eight days. Every now and then he would ask his orhtopaedic expert, when he could return to his acting schedule.

There are people like Mr. S, who are bollywood stars and who loose crores of rupees, if they become victims of fractures, injuries or accidents. They want to get healed fast, so that they back to work and earn crores of rupees.

Case Study No. 14

I Lose my Daily Wages, if I Spend Time with my Husband

Mrs. T, a married female aged 30, having two kids. Her husband met with an accident and broke his tibia. He was admitted in general hospital, Gadchiroli. The orthopaedic surgeon operated, the patient and fixed the bone.

The patient was asked to be in the hospital for 5 to 6 days. His wife Mrs. T, stayed for 2 days and later asked her brother to be in the hospital with her husband. She and her husband were daily wage labourers and landless. She had borrowed four thousand on interest from a money lender.

Mrs. T had extra tension of paying the money borrowed. Moreover, his two kids who were small and were at home. She had to work to earn wages to feed her family, since her husband was admitted.

There are daily wage labourers like Mrs. T, who cannot afford to be with their husbands and take care of them, as they lose their daily wages.

Case Study No. 15

Some Traditional Bone Setters do not Charge Money

Mr. V, aged 54, a male belonging to Mavchi tribe, hails from Navapur block of Nandurbar district, has been setting broken bones since the last 20 years. He gets patients from Gujarat, Madhya Pradesh and Maharashtra states. Most patients of his are poor tribals.

Patients are happy with his treatment and give him Rs. 20 to 100. Sometimes he is given 3 to 5 kilograms of Jowar millet, a bottle of locally prepared Mauha liquor or a coconut. Mr. V does not have fixed rates for treatment.

He says God has given him the skill of setting bones, through his father and hence he does not intend to commercialize it. He accepts whatever amount he gets from people. Rich people sometimes pay him Rs. 1000/-. He takes it.

However, if poor tribal patients come to him he treats them free of cost. Sometimes gives them money for transportation. The moral of the case study is that there are several tribals in India who cannot afford to pay for orthopaedic treatment and hence bone-setters like Mr. V are their saviours.

Analysis of the above mentioned case studies reveal that the phenomena of Health Expenditure and Economics of Muscular-Skeletal Therapy are intertwined with:

1. Social, economic, educational and political status of an individual, family and community members opting for orthopaedic treatment is intertwined with expenditure.

2. That, economically well-off patients with musculo-skeletal disorders tend to avail best of the best treatment and services from reputed orthopaedic hospitals and institutions.
3. That, economically poor patients with musculo-skeletal disorders avail treatment from local bone setters, herbalists and masseurs or prefer to go to government hospitals or live with pain and agony.
4. Borrowing money from relatives, money lenders, taking loan on interest is also linked with musculo-skeletal therapy.
5. That, people take preventive and promotive precautions to maintain and strengthen the growth of their muscles and skeletal system by taking good diet and regular exercises.
6. That, the general public and common man is unaware of the rates and quality of implants, rods, screws etc used for fixing bones for musculo-skeletal disorders.
7. That, the orthopaedic surgeons, hospitals and institutions play a pivotal role in deciding rates for orthopaedic treatment and surgeries.
8. That, rates for muscular-skeletal disorders vary from one region to another.
9. That, when all patients fail to cure a musculo-skeletal disorder, people tend to spend money visiting religious centers, shamans and offerings.

An attempt has been made by the authors to present rates for treatment fractures and surgeries both in government and private hospitals.

COST OF MUSCULO-SKELETAL SURGERIES AND TREATMENT IN PRIVATE AND GOVERNMENT HOSPITALS

It is observed that private hospitals provide better services than the government hospitals and hence charge more to the patients for surgeries, hospitalization, consultation, medicines and physiotherapy. Government hospitals have staff and orthopaedic surgeons who get monthly salary and hence surgery, hospitalization and physiotherapy is free. The patients have to however pay for implants and medicines. Given table 4.1 (*See Table on next page*) that depict rates for a few muscular skeletal surgeries and hospitalization charges in Nagpur city.

Notes

1. The rates given above may vary from hospital to hospital.
2. Rates of medicines and physiotherapy are not included in the above rates.
3. Rates for above surgeries are double in Pune city and three times more in Bombay city.
4. These are major surgeries only.
5. Fracture Acetabulum is a surgery performed by few trained and experienced surgeons only. This surgery requires special training, experience and exposure. Hence, the cost of the fracture fixation of Acetabulum is more as compared to other fracture fixation or surgeries.
6. 90 per cent of the fractures in Paediatric age group are managed by conservative means and do not required surgery.
7. Head injuries are handled by neuro-surgeon only. By and large orthopaedic surgeons do not take up these cases.
8. Clavicle Fractures – 99 per cent of clavicle fractures do not required surgeries. Such fractures are managed conservatively. When the patients demand and if the fracture clavicle is severely displaced, then only the orthopaedic surgeon operates. Clavicle is the only bone transversely present in the human body and therefore, the weight of the body is not transmitted over through this bone. Hence, fracture clavicle requires no surgery. It is only for skeletal support.
9. Surgery in government hospital is performed free of charge. The orthopaedic surgeon charge for implants required for the surgery and hence the rates are less.

Table 4.1: Table Showing Approximate Cost of Orthopaedic Surgeries in Private and Government Hospitals in Nagpur City

Sr. No.	Surgery/Fracture	Rates in Rupees	
		Private Hospital Rates	Government Hospital Rates
1.	Shoulder Surgeries		
(a)	Fracture shaft of humeres, anywhere from upper 3rd to lower 3rd. (Dynamic Compression plating - D.C.P.	30,000.00	5,000.00
(b)	Fracture shaft of humorous anywhere from upper 3rd to middle 3rd (Nailing)	30,000.00	4,000.00
(c)	Stiff shoulder (Neglected shoulder dislocation)	40,000.00	–
2.	Fracture - Supra - condular humeres (Neglected)	50,000.00	5,000.00
3.	Stiff elbow (Neglected elbow dislocation)	35,000.00	–
4.	Fracture Ulna/Radius (Upper 3rd to Lower 3rd D.C.P)	35,000.00	4,000.00
5.	Fracture Ulna/Radius (Upper 3rd to Lower 3rd -Nailing)	20,000.00	1,000.00
6.	Fracture - Lower end of radius (Colles fracture)	20,000.00	2,000.00

(Contd...)

Sr. No.	Surgery/Fracture	Rates in Rupees	
		Private Hospital Rates	Government Hospital Rates
7.	Fractures of the Hip		
(a)	Fracture I.T (Inter-trochiantric fracture)	40,000.00	1,500.00
(b)	Fracture of I.C (Inter-capsular neck femur)	40,000.00	3,000.00
(c)	Fracture Acetabulum	80,000.00	3,000.00
(d)	Fracture (sub-trochiantric)	40,000.00	5,000.00
(e)	Stiff Hip dislocation (Neglected)	40,000.00	5,000.00
(f)	Total Hip replacement surgery	1,30,000.00	65,000.00
(g)	Fracture Shaft Femur (Upper 3rd to Lower 3rd - Nailing)	40,000.00	5,000.00
(h)	Fracture - Distal end of femur (Locking Plate	50,000.00	6,000.00
8.	Knee Joint Surgeries		
(a)	Total knee replacement	1,75,000.00	60,000.00
(b)	Proximal Tibia	40,000.00	5,000.00
(c)	Fracture Tibia (Upper 3rd to Lower 3rd - Nailing)	35,000.00	3,000.00
(d)	Fracture - Distal end of tibia	35,000.00	3,000.00

(Contd…)

Sr. No.	Surgery/Fracture	Rates in Rupees	
		Private Hospital Rates	Government Hospital Rates
9.	Potl's Fracture	40,000.00	1,000.00
10.	Fracture Calcaneum (Heel)	50,000.00	3,000.00
11.	Fractures of the Spine		
(a)	Cervicle Spine	1,20,000.00	10,000.00
(b)	Thorasic Spine	60,000.00	8,000.00
(c)	Lumbar Spine	–	–
(i)	Surgery with implants	70,000.00	10,000.00
(ii)	Surgery without implants	50,000.00	–

(a) Orthopaedics: Advance Deposit for Surgery

In this section of the chapter, the authors have given advance deposit for orthopaedic surgeries of a well known private hospital in Pune. This rate card provides charges for advance deposit only and not full charges. The note given below each card clarifies the extra payment to be made by the patient. The final charges are calculated by the hospital management depending on the type of orthopaedic surgery, the type of ward or room in which the patient is admitted, number of hospitalization days, the treatment and medicines prescribed, the type of physiotherapy exercises recommended while in the hospital etc.

Orthopaedics: Advance Deposit for Surgery

Sr. No.	Surgery Name	Gen. Ward	Semi – Spl/ICU	Spl. Room/ Nursing
1	2	3	4	5
1.	Plate & screw fixation fracture Tibia	10,500	14,600	19,700
2.	Plate & screw fixation fracture Tibia + bone graft	15,600	21,700	29,300
3.	Plate & screws fixation fracture calcaneous	10,500	14,600	19,700
4.	Plate & screws fixation fracture calcaneous + bone graft	15,600	21,700	29,300
5.	Plate & screws fixation fracture clavicle	10,500	14,600	19,700
6.	Plate & screws fixation fracture clavicle + bone graft	15,600	21,700	29,300
7.	Plate & screw fixation fracture Fibula and medial melleolus	12,600	17,500	23,600
8.	Plate & screw fixation fracture Fibula and medial melleolus + bone graft	17,900	24,900	33,700
9.	Plate & screw fixation fracture tibial condyles	12,600	17,500	23,600
10.	Plate & screw fixation fracture tibial condyles + bone graft	17,900	24,900	33,700

(Contd...)

1	2	3	4	5
11.	Plate & screws fixation fracture acetabulum	14,500	20,100	27,200
12.	Plate & screws fixation metacarpals fractures	6,500	9,100	12,200
13.	Putti-Plat operation	12,600	17,500	23,600
14.	Radius and Ulna nailing with bone grafting – Double	15,600	21,700	29,300
15.	Radius and Ulna nailing with bone grafting – Single	14,500	20,100	27,200
16.	Radius/Ulna Dynamic compression plating (DCP) – Double	12,600	17,500	23,600
17.	Radius/Ulna Dynamic compression plating (DCP) – Single	10,500	14,600	19,700
18.	Radius/Ulna Dynamic compression plating (DCP) + bone graft – Single	12,600	17,500	23,600
19.	Radius/Ulna Dynamic compression plating (DCP) + bone graft – Double	18,900	26,300	35,500
20.	Reconstruction fracture lower end Humures + Tension Band Olecranon	18,900	26,300	35,500
21.	Reconstruction fracture lower end Humeres	14,500	20,100	27,200
22.	Reduction of compound fractures plus suturing charges	3,600	5,000	6,800
23.	Release Dequervian's Disease (Tenosynovitis Thumb)	4,600	6,400	8,600
24.	Release of Carpel Tunnel Syndrome	6,500	9,100	12,200
25.	Release Trigger Finger	5,400	7,500	10,200
26.	Removal/Readjustment External Fixator	3,600	5,000	6,800
27.	Removal of Humeres plate and screws	5,400	7,500	10,200
28.	Removal of inter locking nail	8,400	11,700	15,800
29.	Removal of 'K' wires after exploration	3,600	5,000	6,800
30.	Removal of nail femur/tibia/humeres	5,400	7,500	10,200
31.	Removal of Percutaneous 'K' wires	2,800	3,900	5,200

(Contd...)

1	2	3	4	5
32.	Removal of plate and screws Femur/Tibia	5,400	7,500	10,200
33.	Removal of plate and screws ankle (per site i.e. Tibia & Fibula)	5,400	7,500	10,200
34.	Removal of plate and screws from fracture neck Humerus	5,400	7,500	10,200
35.	Removal of Radius & Ulna nails (Double)	5,400	7,500	10,200
36.	Removal of Radius plate and screws	5,400	7,500	10,200
37.	Removal of Ulna and Radius plate & screws	5,400	7,500	10,200
38.	Removal of Ulna nail/Radius nail (Single)	3,600	5,000	6,800
39.	Removal of Ulna plate and screws	5,400	7,500	10,200
40.	Revision cup in THR	18,900	26,300	35,500
41.	Revision cup + stem in THR	35,000	48,600	65,800
42.	Revision stem in THR	18,900	26,300	35,500
43.	Rush nailing fracture Humerus	9,500	13,300	17,900
44.	Skeletal traction + fracture reduction	4,600	6,400	8,600
45.	Soutte's Release (Flexion contracture Hip in Polio)	6,500	9,100	12,200
46.	Spinal fusion	17,900	24,900	33,700
47.	Steffi plate – Screw fixation fracture spine (any implant fixator)	25,800	35,800	48,400
48.	Strapping of joints & Fractures	2,500	3,500	4,700
49.	Sub-Trochanteric Osteotomy femur with fixation	10,500	14,600	19,700
50.	Supracondylar Osteotomy femur with fixation	10,500	14,600	19,700
51.	Supracondylar Osteotomy Humerus with fixation	10,500	14,600	19,700
52.	Surgical repair recurrent dislocation Patella	12,600	17,500	23,600
53.	Synovectomy	10,500	14,600	19,700

(Contd…)

1	2	3	4	5
54.	Tendo-Achillis Lengthening	6,500	9,100	12,200
55.	Tendo-Achillis Lengthening with Extensor Proneus Hallusis to M I	8,400	11,700	15,800
56.	Tension Band wiring Acromio – Clavicular dislocation	10,500	14,600	19,700
57.	Tension Band wiring Fracture medial malleolus/lateral malleolus	10,500	14,600	19,700
58.	Tension Band wiring fracture patella	10,500	14,600	19,700
59.	Tension Band wiring Olecraneon/trochanter	10,500	14,600	19,700
60.	Tibial Pin Traction	4,600	6,400	8,600
61.	Total Hip replacement	30,800	42,900	58,000
62.	Total Knee replacement	30,800	42,900	58,000
63.	Total Shoulder replacement	30,800	42,900	58,000
64.	Triple arthrodosis	15,600	21,700	29,300
65.	Trochanteric Pin Traction	4,600	6,400	8,600
66.	Wrist arthrodosis	12,600	17,500	23,600
67.	Yount's release (Flexion contracture knee)	5,400	7,500	10,200
68.	Pelvic Support Osteotomy + Bone Grafting + Plating	20,900	29,100	39,400
69.	Excision of lower end of Ulna	10,500	14,600	19,700
70.	Bipolar Hip Replacement Modular Cemented	27,800	38,700	52,300
71.	Proximal Femur Nailing	24,800	34,500	46,600
72.	Partial Shoulder Replacement	25,800	35,800	48,400
73.	Reaming of Medular cavity for osteomyelities of long bones	11,500	15,900	21,500
74.	Cosyotransversectomy with Anterio-Lateral decompression	24,800	34,500	46,600
75.	ACL Reconstruction	21,900	30,500	41,200

Note:

1. Anaesthetist charges would be @ 30% of Surgeon's fees.
2. Advance Deposit @ 260% (Gen. Ward), 240% (Semi-Spl.) and 210% (Spl. Room and NH) of Surgeon's Fees.
3. Surgeon's fees are fixed irrespective of No. of Surgeons.

(b) Physiotherapy Charges

In this section of the book an effort has been made to provide charges for physiotherapy of the same private hospital with effect from 1st April, 2011. These charges are on the basis of type of ward a patient is admitted in. In case of Out Patient Department, charges are separate. The table given below throws light on the same.

Sr. No.	Particulars	OPD	Gen. Ward	Semi–Spl/ICU	Special Room/ Nursing Home
1	2	3	4	5	6
1.	**Exercises:**				
	General	90.00	100.00	120.00	140.00
	Neuro or more than ½ hr.	90.00	100.00	120.00	140.00
2.	Electrotherapy Modalities				
(a)	S.W.D (Short Wave Diathermy)	90.00	100.00	120.00	140.00
(b)	Infra Red	90.00	100.00	120.00	140.00
(c)	Ultrasound Therapy	90.00	100.00	120.00	140.00
3.	Intermittent Cervical/ Lumbar Traction	100.00	110.00	130.00	150.00
4.	Ankle Traction	90.00	100.00	120.00	140.00
5.	Wax Bath (Paraffin)	90.00	100.00	120.00	140.00
6.	Interferential Therapy	110.00	120.00	140.00	165.00
7.	Electric Muscles Stimulation	90.00	100.00	120.00	140.00
8.	Gait Training	80.00	90.00	100.00	120.00
9.	Hot Pack Therapy	90.00	100.00	120.00	140.00
10.	Chest P.T.				
(a)	Breathing Exercises	80.00	90.00	100.00	120.00
(b)	Postural Drainage	80.00	90.00	100.00	120.00
11.	Continuous Passive Mobilizer				
(a)	½ Hour	90.00	100.00	120.00	140.00
(b)	Full day	110.00	120.00	140.00	165.00
12.	Exercise – Demonstration	80.00	90.00	100.00	120.00

(Contd...)

1	2	3	4	5	6
13.	Laser Therapy	110.00	120.00	140.00	165.00
14.	Physiotherapy Evaluation	80.00	90.00	100.00	120.00
15.	Pre and Post natal exercises	80.00	90.00	100.00	120.00
16.	Wheel Chair Mobilization	90.00	100.00	120.00	140.00
17.	TENS (Transcutaneous Electric Nerve Stimulation)	90.00	100.00	120.00	140.00
18.	Muscle Charting	90.00	100.00	120.00	140.00
19.	Tread Mill Exercise (TMT) – per ½ hr. or part thereof	110.00	120.00	140.00	165.00

(c) Kerala Ayurvedic treatment: Approximate Costing

In recent years the Kerala Ayurvedic Treatment has become popular world over, because of its efficacy. A Pamphlet published by the Jeevana Holistic Health Centre, Pune, Maharashtra, India states that, "It's amazing that Ayurveda, the five thousand year old science of life, is relevant still today. It is the world's first and completely natural medical system, developed by ancient masters and physicians. In Ayurveda the focus is on uprooting the disease and empowering the immune system, rather than respected and used worldwide. In today's hectic lifestyle, Ayurveda has gained special significance.

The Jeevana Health Centre at Pune activates the inherent curative powers of the body and mind through the right approach to life. Some of the therapies and facilities provided by the Jeevana Health Centre are:

1. Relaxation, rejuvenation and health preservation therapies.
2. Ayurvedic full body massage to recharge your body, mind and soul.
3. Special stress bursting massage for IT/BPO/Business Executives.
4. Beauty treatment of skin, hair and figure development.
5. Hot oil therapies, medical steam, herbal diet, Ayurvedic medicines, yoga, meditation etc.

6. Consultation by expert doctors from Kerala.

The centre also offers specific Kerala Ayurvedic Treatment for different types of diseases, namely:

1. **Rheumatoid Arthritis** – Pizhichil (oil bath)
2. **Osteo-Arthritis** – Kizhi
3. **Muscular Dystrophy** – Navara Kizhi
4. **Sciatica, Slip Disc, Backache etc** – Kativasthi
5. **Frozen Shoulder** – Nasyam
6. **Facial Paralysis & Disorders affecting the Cranial Nerve** – Shirovasthi

The rates quoted by the centre as on November, 2012 are as below:

1. Oil Therapy – Rs. 2000/-
2. Dhura Therapy – Rs. 1500/-
3. Rotli Therapy – Rs. 1500/-
4. Milk Therapy – Rs. 1500/-

The entire package with discount works out to Rs. 3500/-

(d) Discussion

Charges regarding orthopaedic surgeries vary from hospital to hospital. These charges keep fluctuating. The type and class of facility, hospital environment, consultation, experience name and fame of the orthopaedic surgeon who performs the surgery etc play an important role in fixing charges. People opt for the class and type of hospital and treatment depending on their ability to pay for orthopaedic treatment.

SOCIO-ECONOMIC STATUS OF FAMILIES THAT OPT FOR GOVERNMENT HOSPITAL TREATMENT

The authors of this book carried out a survey of 100 indoor patients with muscular-skeletal disorders in General Government Hospital, Gadchiroli, keeping in view following objectives.

1. To study the social, educational and economic background of the patients and their families.

2. To understand the health expenditure pattern with reference to muscular-skeletal disorders.
3. To explore the aspect of borrowing loan and money for treatment.

A survey form was designed to gather relevant data and 100 patients were interviewed during the year 2011-2012. The major findings of the survey are as below:

1. **Age range of the patients:** The survey revealed that –
   - 45 per cent of the patients belonged to pediatric age group ie; from 0 to 18 years.
   - 30 per cent belonged to the age range 18.5 to 35 years.
   - 16 per cent belonged to the age group 35.5 to 50 years.
   - 8 per cent belonged to the age group 50.5 to 70 years.
2. **Sex of the Patients**

Out of the total 100 patients surveyed 71 per cent were males and 29 per cent were females.

3. **Caste/Tribe status**

Out of the total 100 patients 26 per cent belonged to Scheduled Tribe,40 per cent to Scheduled Castes, 24 per cent to Other Backward Classes and 10 per cent to Upper Castes.

4. **Occupation of the father**

Table 4.2 reveals the occupation of fathers of patients or household heads or patient themselves.

Table 4.2: Occupation of the Patient's Father

Sr. No.	Occupation	Number	Percentage
1.	Small Scale Cultivators	47	47%
2.	Agriculture Labourers	21	21%
3.	Daily Wage Labourers	12	12%
4.	Small Scale Business	02	2%
5.	Government Service	08	8%
6.	Private Service	10	10%
	Total	**100**	**100%**

It is evident from table 4.2 that 47 per cent of the father's of the patients are small scale cultivators, 21 per cent agriculture labourers, 12 per cent daily wage labourers, 2 per cent were engaged in small scale business, while 18 per cent were in government and private service.

5. **Status of Land Holding**

Table 4.3 reveals the status of land holding of the 100 respondents interviewed.

Table 4.3: Status of Land Holding

Sr. No.	Land Holding	Number	Percentage
1.	Landless	53	53%
2.	Land Holders	47	47%
	Total	100	100%

As evident from table 4.3, the survey revealed that 53 per cent of the respondent families were landless, while 47 per cent were small scale land holders.

6. **Land holding in acres**

The survey revealed that out of the 47 land holders 31 per cent had agricultural land less than one acre, 59 per cent possessed between 1½ to 5 acres and 10 per cent had land above 5 acres.

7. **Annual Income of the family**

Table 4.4 reveals the annual income of the respondent families.

Table 4.4: Annual Income of the Family

Sr. No.	Income Range	Number	Percentage
1.	Less than 20,000/-	50	50%
2.	Rs. 20,001 to 40,000/-	24	24%
3.	Rs. 40,001 to 60,000/-	6	6%
4.	Rs. 60,001 to 80,000/-	3	3%
5.	Rs. 80,001 to 1 Lakh	8	8%
6.	Above 1 Lakh	9	9%
	Total	100	100%

Figures in table 4.4 reveal that 50 per cent of the families were below the poverty line. 24 per cent earned between Rs. 20,001 to 40,000 per annum, while 26 per cent earned above 40,001 rupees per annum.

8. **Size of the family**

The survey revealed that 2 per cent of the respondents had a size of 2 members; 48 per cent between 2 to 4, 33 per cent between 4 to 6, and 17 per cent above 6 members.

9. **Expenditure on orthopaedic treatment**

Table 4.5, presents the status of expenditure on orthopaedic treatment in the government hospital.

Table 4.5: Expenditure on Treatment

Sr. No.	Expense Range	Number	Percentage
1.	Less than Rs. 3000/-	33	33%
2.	Rs. 3001 to 5000/-	36	36%
3.	Rs. 5001 to 10,000/-	21	21%
4.	Rs. 10,001 to 20,000/-	07	7%
5.	Above 20,001	03	3%
	Total	**100**	**100%**

As evident from table number 4.5 33 per cent of respondents spend less than Rs. 3000/-; 36 per cent spend between Rs. 3001 to 5000/-; 21 per cent between Rs. 5001 to 10,000/-; 7 per cent between Rs. 10,001 to 20,000/- and 3 per cent above Rs. 20,001. It was observed that this expenditure included money for purchasing implants for surgery or fixing bones, medicines, special diet for patients and transportation.

10. **Source of loan taken**

Table 4.6 reveals that 47 per cent of the patients borrowed loan or money with or without interest from relatives, friends and money lenders, while 38 per cent spend from personal or family's savings; 8 per cent borrowed from employer and 5 per cent took money from their General Provident Fund.

Table 4.6: Source of Loan taken for Treatment

Sr. No.	Source of Loan	Number	Percentage
1.	Personal/Family's Savings	38	38%
2.	Relatives	10	10%
3.	Friends	05	5%
4.	Money Lenders	32	32%
5.	Bank	—	—
6.	General Provident Fund	05	5%
7.	Employer	08	8%
8.	Others	02	2%
	Total	**100**	**100%**

11. **Educational status**

Out of the 100 patients interviewed 43 per cent were illiterate, 27 per cent studied up till primary, 11 per cent up to high school, 8 up to graduation, 8 per cent up to masters and 3 per cent did not respond.

The statistical data projected through the survey conducted in a Government Hospital of one of the most backward and sensitive districts such as Gadchiroli reveal that there are socio-economically backward people who cannot afford to take treatment in private orthopaedic hospitals. That, most of them borrowed money with or without interest from relatives, friends and money lenders for treatment. Dr. Satish Meshram, Senior Orthopaedic Surgeon and co-author of this book states that he has come across many poor patients, who cannot afford to purchase implants and hence go back to the traditional bone setters. It is observed that the traditional bone setters and orthopaedic surgeons in government hospitals are only saviours of poor people in remote tribal and rural areas.

HOW MANY ORTHOPAEDIC SURGEONS WORK IN GOVERNMENT HOSPITALS OF GADCHIROLI, BHANDARA AND GONDIYA DISTRICTS?

The present research has established the fact that poor people cannot afford orthopaedic treatment in private hospitals because of heavy fees, and hence they opt to go to government hospitals and traditional bone setters. If public health is the responsibility of the state, are there enough government orthopaedic hospitals, surgeons and qualified staff in a remote and sensitive district such as Gadchiroli? This question not only haunts the mind of a common man, doctors, policy makers but health administrators as well. The table given below presents statistics of orthopaedic hospitals, units and surgeons in government general and rural hospitals in Gadchiroli district.

Table 4.7: Status of Orthopaedic Units and Surgeons in Government Hospitals and PHC's in Gadchiroli District

Sr. No.	Hospitals/PHC's	Total No.	No. of Orthopaedic Units	No. of Orthopaedic Surgeons
1.	General/Civil Hospitals	1	1	2
2.	Rural Hospitals	13	–	–
3.	Primary Health Centers	45	–	–
4.	Primary Health Units	36	–	–
5.	Municipal Corporation Hospitals	–	–	–
6.	Municipality Hospitals	–	–	–
7.	Police Hospitals	1	–	–
8.	Sub-centres	376	–	–
	Total	**472**	**1**	**2**

Source: D.H.O & Civil Surgeon, Gadchiroli as on 10/09/12.

It is clear from the table 4.7 that there are only two Government Orthopaedic Surgeons in the entire Gadchiroli district. These two surgeons are employed in the general hospital in Gadchiroli. It is pertinent to note that the police hospital in Gadchiroli does not have an orthopaedic surgeon. Being s sensitive-naxal affected district there are cases of bombing and injuries due to encounters with Naxals etc. Hence, recruiting an orthopaedic surgeon and establishing a fully equipped trauma unit in the police hospital, is a must. Further, it is recommended that even the rural hospitals should have trained and experienced orthopaedic surgeons. Similar situation was observed by the authors in Bhandara and Gondiya districts, which are sensitive and Naxal affected. Tables 4.8 and 4.9 reveal the factual position in these two districts.

Table 4.8: Status of Orthopaedic Units and Surgeons in Government Hospitals and P.H.C's in Bhandara District

Sr. No.	Hospitals/PHC's	Total No.	No. of Orthopaedic Units	No. of Orthopaedic Surgeons
1.	General/Civil Hospitals	1	1	
2.	Rural Hospitals	7	–	–
3.	Primary Health Centers	33	–	–
4.	Primary Health Units	2	–	–
5.	Municipal Corporation Hospitals	–	–	–
6	Municipality Hospitals	–	–	–
7.	Police Hospitals	–	–	–
8.	Sub-centres	193	–	–
9.	Dispensaries	29	–	–
	Total			

Source: D.H.O & Civil Surgeon Offices, Bhandara as on 06/10/12.

LESS TRAINED AND EXPERIENCED ORTHOPAEDIC SURGEONS IN RURAL AREAS: A SERIOUS HEALTHCARE CONCERN

Informal discussions with orthopaedic surgeons practicing privately as well as those working in government hospitals, revealed that there hardly any orthopaedic surgeons, who wish to join government service, especially to work in remote and sensitive districts like Gadchiroli, Gondiya, Bhandara etc. Most of them prefer practicing privately because:

1. They get more income in private practice.
2. They are free from the government norms and regulations of service.
3. In private practice, they are progressive in their profession and have scope to do research, attend conferences, seminars, go abroad for short courses and exposure visits etc.

Table 4.9: Status of Orthopaedic Units and Surgeons in Government Hospitals and P.H.C's in Gondiya District

Sr. No.	Hospitals/PHC's	Total No.	No. of Orthopaedic Units	No. of Orthopaedic Surgeons
1.	General/Civil Hospitals	1	1	3
2.	Rural Hospitals	11	–	–
3.	Primary Health Centers	39	–	–
4.	Primary Health Units	1	–	–
5.	Municipal Corporation Hospitals	–	–	–
6.	Municipality Hospitals	–	–	–
7.	Police Hospitals	–	–	–
8.	Sub-centres	237	–	–
9.	Dispensaries	39	–	–
10.	Women's Hospitals	01	–	–
	Total	**1**	**3**	

Source: D.H.O & Civil Surgeon Offices, Gondiya as on 06/10/12.

Well, that is the interpretation of the orthopaedic surgeons. This does not mean people in the rural and tribal areas suffering from injuries, accidents and musculo-skeletal disorders, should be deprived of healthcare and facilities.

There is an urgent need to think about the need to recruit experienced and trained orthopaedic surgeons and other medical staff in the district trauma centers, general hospitals and even in rural hospitals and sub-district hospitals. Efforts should be made to give extra financial incentives to trained and experienced orthopaedic surgeons.

SHIFT IN MUSCULAR-SKELETAL THERAPY

In their paper captioned, "Ethno-Medical Pathway: A Conceptual Model", Tribhuwan Robin and Gambir R.D (1995), have revealed that if treatment is sought on the basis of initial diagnosis, proves ineffective, patients then shift from one therapy to another. This trend of shifting from one therapy to another during illness progression was observed among four tribes.

In his study, among the Baluhis of Central India, Fuchs Stephen (1964: 122-24) states that, the Baluhis are aware of the fact that certain diseases have natural causes and so they first look for natural remedies to cure them by resorting to household medicine, when these medicines fail to cure an illness, friends and relatives send their advise that certain deity or spirit has been offended and has sent the illness in revenge. Hence a Janka (herbalist – cum – diviner) or Badwa (Shaman) is consulted.

This trend of shifting from one therapy to another during the illness progression of muscular-skeletal disorders was observed by the authors of this book. Patients attended by bone setters, go to an orhtopaedic surgeon, or a masseur or ayurvedic practitioner. Similarly, patients attended by an orthopaedic surgeon go to the traditional bone setter, a masseur or ayurvedic practitioner.

In his study, "Medical World of Tribals", Tribhuwan Robin (1998), has identified various reasons for shifting from one therapy to another. These are as follows:

1. The prolonged duration of illness and patients expectations to get quick results.
2. At times, what may be initially attributed to have caused or originated due to intervention of supernatural beings or forces. This would change the course of treatment from one to another therapy.
3. Thirdly, if a therapy or treatment is found ineffective the patient would try another therapy.

THE ECONOMICS OF PHYSIOTHERAPY

Physiotherapy is a healthcare profession concerned with human function and movement and maximizing potential. It uses physical approaches to promote, maintain and restore physical, psychological and social well being, taking into account variations in health status. It is science-based, committed to extending, applying, evaluating and reviewing the evidence that underpins and uniforms the practice and delivery. The exercise of clinical judgement and informed interpretation is its core. (CSP, 2002, b)

In their paper captioned, "The responsibilities of being a physiotherapist, Hammond Ralph and Wheeler Julie (2009:1) have stated that physiotherapists came into the profession because they have an underlying sense and commitment to helping others and improving their quality of life.

Koehn D. (1994) argues that professionals can be thought of being defined by a distinctive commitment to benefit the client. The role of a physiotherapist is certainly very important in orthopaedic treatment. They say that an orthopaedic surgeon performs a successful surgery, but the success of his surgery depends a lot on the physiotherapy.

Writing about the significance of physiotherapy in low backache treatment, Ebnezar John (2012:61) stated that, this is an important method of treatment and you may use it to support drug treatment or during post surgical recovery. Sometimes in certain extraordinary situations it may form the main stay of treatment. The following are some of the commonly recommended physiotherapy methods of treatment.

(a) **Heat Therapy:** Heat helps to increase the blood circulation to the skin, muscles, bones and joints. This increased blood supply takes away the pain producing substances from the tissues and rid you of the pain. Hot water packs and infra red rays help in heating the superficial structures like skin and sub-cutaneous tissues. Ultra sound and short wave diathermy helps in heating deeper structures like muscles, ligaments, bones and joints.

(b) **Cold Therapy:** This consists of the ice pack, ice massage, cold water packs etc. This is very effective when used within first 24 hours of acute injury of the back. After 24-48 hours one can switch over to the heat therapy as mentioned above. Here the mechanism of action is the same as heat therapy.

(c) **Traction:** This method consists of applying pulling forces over the muscles, ligaments, bones and joints with the help of pulling devices. This includes relaxation of muscles and ligaments, separates the bones and the joints and thus helps in reduction of pain and muscle spasm. It serves sone other very important function, that is it ensures that one stays on the bed completely during the treatment period and thereby get all important bed rest in strict sense of the term.

(d) **Massage:** This has been very common method of treating backache since ages. Our fore fathers and ancient physicians prided themselves in this art of treatment. Even in the present era, if done skillfully massage provides a soothing effect and induces relaxation of ones spine muscles and ligaments. It is a very popular method of treatment in our country, and is least expensive, yet effective form of back therapy.

Not all people can afford to take physiotherapy treatment, especially in hospitals and orthopaedic institutions, for it costs money.

ECONOMICS OF DOCTOR – PATIENT RELATIONS

Robert Albert (1958: 506-516) has discussed the issue of economics of doctor – patient relationships. He has stated that a patient who cannot afford to pay anything for medical care is a true indigent. This is the pauper. He further reports that there are very less true indigents in America. Robert Albert argues that the individual doctor must make up his mind whether or not he should treat a poor patient.

The very root of most difficulties between doctors – patient are not those of clinical nature, but rather those involving non – clinical treatment. The most common difficulty between the doctor and patient relation is the bill – the fee for the services performed.

He further argues that people choose a doctor because of the way he treats them, not solely his clinical treatment, but also his treatment of them as individuals. A great deal of treatment as individuals is reflected in his fees and his bill.

Doctors practice medicine to make a profit, because they like their field, because they are needed, and because they obtain personal satisfaction in easing pain and bring comfort to the afflicted. Making a profit does not detract them from the merits of higher motives. If a physician fails to make profit, then it becomes extremely difficult to practice good medicine. (Robert Albright 1958).

The entire debate of the economics of doctor – patient relationship revolves around quality health services and the payment of fees as per the standard of quality health services. It is pertinent to note at this juncture is that there are people who can afford to pay in lakhs, for quality health services, comfort and health restoration is their criteria.

On the other hand there are true indigents – patients who cannot afford to pay for medical care and hence choose to go to the traditional medical practitioners, including the bone setters or government hospitals for that matter. In India, the percentage of true indigents is high, and needs to be tackled efficiently, if health has to be given to all by 2020 or even 2050 as it were.

5

Growth of Bones and Muscles *Ethno-nutritional Beliefs and Practices*

BODY IMAGE: A SYMBOLIC INTERPRETATION

Before getting into understanding people's beliefs, values, perceptions, knowledge and understanding regarding their concept of growth of muscles and bones and the role of diet in promoting the same, it is necessary to brief the readers of this book, with human body symbolism.

BODY IMAGE

Use of human body as a symbolic material has been discussed by Anthropologists and analyzed in allied disciplines. (Joshi 1992:9) As a symbolic instrument a person may use his body as a means of communication, to indicate by bodily actions or with reference to some more abstract idea which is meaningful to him and his community.

As Mauss puts it, "the human body is the first and the most natural instrument of man (1950:372). Human body as a symbolic instrument conveys meaning and is used as means of communication. Meanings of bodily symbols are situationally defined and expressed within cultural context.

Many Douglas (1970:65) states that the social body constrains the way the physical body is perceived. The physical experience of the body is always modified by the social categories through which it is known, sustains a particular view of the society. That, there is a continual exchange of meanings between the two kinds of bodily experiences so that each reinforces the categories of others.

In his book captioned, "Medical World of Tribals", Tribhuwan Robin (1998:164-199) presents the perceptions of Thakur Scheduled Tribe from Maharashtra, India, regarding how human body is defined as a natural, social, spiritual and cosmological symbol situationally expressed in different cultural contexts. Given below are few examples of the same, from the Thakur Scheduled Tribe Community.

Thus, depending on the people's belief regarding the origin and cause of illness, the body of that patient expresses social, spiritual, cosmological, ancestral, evil symbolic form, within a given ritual or cultural context.

Both Turner (1966) and Douglas Mary (1970) have discussed the use of body and bodily emission as non-verbal categories in society. In fact Devisch, Renaat (1985:693) has shown how the northern yak; construct a meaningful world by reference to human body. They understand the socio-cultural domains in terms of bodily exchanges such as ingestion, excretion, sexual process or listening and speech. The physical body as a tangible form of selfhood is the frame through which, spiritual, cosmological paradoxes are expressed.

The state of ill-health, hence situationally defines and expresses people's perceptions of human body as social, spiritual, evil, cosmological or supernatural symbol within a given context.

For example, C haphekar L.N. (1960:82) reveals how Thakur Scheduled Tribals classify ten bodily openings as ten doors. He states that the "secret door" is supposed to be the apex of the scalp of the human skull. The Thakur's believe that the soul (atma) leaves the body, through the secret door.

Table 5.1: Human Body as a Natural, Social, Spiritual, Ancestral and Cosmological Symbol

Sr. No.	Physical Bodily Condition	Symbolic Expression
1	2	3
1.	Shamans (Bhagats) in trance	1. A Shaman in trance during a healing or religious ritual, loses his identity as a human being and becomes a symbol of a divine being, god or goddess and declares the wrong deeds of the Thakur's and the rituals to patch up with the spiritual pathogenic agent.
2.	A person possessed with evil spirit	2. A person who is possessed with an evil spirit loses his social identity. His body is believed to have been controlled by an evil spirit. Thus, his body becomes a symbol of evil spirit.
3.	Chicken Pox	3. The Thakur's believe that "Lahanya Baya" (Junior Female Spirits) visit the body of a patient suffering from chicken pox and hence perform rituals to appease them. Infections and pills are a taboo here. The body of a chicken pox patient hence becomes a symbol of "Junior Female Spirits" situationally.
4.	Small Pox	4. Although, Small Pox has been eradicated, the Thakur's believed that it was caused by the visitation of "Mothya Baya" (Senior Female Planetary Spirits). The body of a Small Pox patient thus became a symbol of cosmic beings. Female planetary spirits meant, the eight planets (sisters) of mother earth.

(Contd...)

1	2	3
5.	An Albino	5. The body of an albino is believed to be a progeny of a white coloured evil spirit called Munja (Chaphekar 1961 & Tribhuwan 1998). This white evil spirit has sexual intercourse with a normal woman and hence an albino child is given birth to. The traditional mid wife with the permission of the family kills the child by choking throat or by suffocation method, by putting a basket smeared with cow dung on the child. The albino's body is situationally a symbol of a white coloured evil spirit.
6.	A patient with fever, believed to be victim of wrath of Ancestral Spirits.	6. Soon after the death of an elderly man or woman in the family, if a child gets fever, the Thakur's believe that the cause of his fever is wrath of ancestral spirits. His body then becomes a symbol of an ancestral spirit.

Tribhuwan Robin (1998) has pointed out that if the eyes or mouth of the deceased are open; the Thakur's believe that the atma has left the body through the mouth or eyes.

Tribhuwan Robin (1998) has revealed these ten doors of the body as believed by Thakur's are eyes, nostrils, mouth, ears, space below the sternum, naval region, urethral and/or vagina opening, and opening and the tenth opening as the apex of the scalp of the skull.

SKELETAL SYSTEM – PEOPLE'S VIEW

Tribhuwan Robin (1998) has shown how Thakur's associate skeletal system (sapla) with a tree having a trunk and various branches. That, the growth of these bones according to the Thakur's depend on food, water, air, fire or heat in the body. The Thakur's believe that the soul (atma) of a tree is in its roots, so also the atma of a human beings is below the sternum surrounded by the cage called ribs.

The Mavchi tribe of Nandurbar believe that meat of goat, chicken and eggs of a hen from rural area are extremely good for the growth of human bones and flesh. (Tomar Y.P.S and Tribhuwan Robin 2005)

The Madia and Gonds of Vidarbha believe that the meat of monitor lizard is good for joint paint, arthritis and growth of muscles and bones (Kurian J.C, Tribhuwan Robin and Meshram Satish, 2012)

Jain N.S and Tribhuwan Robin (1996) have stated that the Karkus believe that skeletal system is the main frame of the human body. That, this frame deteriorates as one grows old. The skeletal system of an elderly person is weak and feeble as compared to a young person.

The Mavchi tribals co-relate the strength of bones of the skeletal system with the thickness of human blood. People with think blood or watery blood have weak bones or skeletal system. Human beings with thick blood are believed to have strong bones.

Informal interviews with ten Gond midwives of Gadchiroli revealed that the bones of a foetus in womb are fully formed in the sixth month of pregnancy. They further stated that bones of the children are tender and in growing stage. People between the age group 20 to 40 have strong bones. After the age of 40 bones start deteriorating with the process of aging. The skeletal system, they stated is the foundation of human body. A person's life becomes difficult if he or she fractures his or her bones. Well, these are people's views about skeletal system and bones. Let us look into people's beliefs about ethno-nutritional beliefs and practices.

WHAT IS ETHNO-NUTRITION ?

Indigenous Knowledge regarding food, its nature, the intrinsic qualities it has, and its hot and cold nature, the impact food has an human physiology and anatomy varies from one society to another.

Nitcher and Nitcher (1981:75) have pointed out that the elaborate and detailed belief systems and underlying food habits in traditional societies are often over looked by the medical personnel.

Ethno-nutrition is defined as those beliefs and practices which are products of indigenous cultural development and are not explicitly derived from the conceptual framework of modern medicine. Thus, even before the advent of modern medicine people developed historically learnt and culturally shared beliefs and practices regarding:

1. What food is ?
2. What nutrition is ?
3. The intrinsic qualities of food ?
4. Classification of non-vegetarian and vegetarian food.
5. Hot and cold qualities of food and its impact on body physiology and anatomy.
6. Food as medicine.
7. Food that is hard to digest and those foods that are easy to digest.
8. Impact of stale food on the digestive system.
9. Fruits, vegetables, pulses, cereals, nuts, meat, milk etc that contribute to the purification of blood.

10. Food that contributes to the growth and strengthening of human bodily organs.
11. Food that aggravates disease.
12. Wrong combination of diet leading to disease.
13. Foods that are harmful to human body.
14. Foods that contribute to the growth and strengthening of muscles and bones.

Some of the areas of ethno-nutrition according to us are:

1. People's definition and classification of food.
2. People's perceptions regarding the nutritional, medicinal, hot and cold and harmful qualities of food, and their impact on human body.
3. People's beliefs and practices regarding dietary habits.
4. Beliefs and practices regarding what foods should be given to an infant, a child, a pregnant woman and a new mother, a sick and old person, to a wrestler and a sportsman etc.
5. People's concept of food taste and satisfaction.
6. Beliefs and practices regarding consumption of food quantity in different seasons.
7. Perception regarding fasting and body maintenance.
8. People's perception about how food gets converted into blood and nutrients.

It is essential at this juncture to give examples of the above classified areas of ethno-nutrition:

1. **People's definition and classification of food.**
   (a) **Definition of food:** The concept and definition of food varies from one society to another. For some societies cooked and or baked cereals, pulses, meat, vegetables, beans etc include food. For some society's raw fruits, leaves, vegetables, seeds, partially cooked or fried meat includes food.

There are those societies that believe in consuming raw as well as cooked food that is edible and digestable.

(b) **Classification of Food**

(i) **Hot and Cold Foods**

Most caste, tribal and nomadic communities in India classifies food into temperature and chilly hot foods. However, cold foods are temperature cold foods. For example; hot milk, tea, coffee, curry, rice, bread etc are temperature hot foods. Whereas curd, ice-cream, Luke warm, Jowar roti are temperature cold foods. Food with excess chilly are chilly hot foods.

(ii) **Hard and Light Food**

Food that hard to digest is classified as "Jad Anna" (hard food), while food that is light (halka anna) is classified as soft food. Thus, meat, chicken, dry fish, raw cereals, pulses, seeds etc are believed to be hard foods. Whereas fruits, vegetables, baked bread, milk, curds, porridge etc are believed to be light foods.

(iii) **Cooked and Raw Foods**

As the title suggests people believe that there is cooked as well as raw food.

2. **People's perceptions regarding intrinsic qualities of food.**

People world over believe that food has healing, nourishing, hot, cold and strengthening qualities. Thus, turmeric powder taken with milk or curry is believed to heal internal cuts, boils or wounds of intestines and other organs of the digestive system.

Ricinus Communis (Erand) seed oil mixed with food and taken in small quantity is believed to clean up the digestive system. Juice of Neem leaves (Azadrachta Indica) is believed to control sugar and diabetes. Meat and chicken soup strengthens bones and muscles.

3. **People's beliefs and practices regarding dietary habits.**

Goans, Bengalis, Kokani people cannot enjoy a meal without fish. The castes and tribes of Vidarbha compulsorily include chilly in their diet. The Thakur's, Katkari's, Warli's, Kolidhar's of Western Maharashtra love to have a meal with dry fish. People from Andhra Pradesh, Kerala, Tamil Nadu and Karnataka cannot think of a meal without rice.

Similarly, the Punjabi's cannot dream of a meal without tandoori roti, nan or a paratha. People in Kolhapur district have the habit of having "Safed Rassa" (white meat flavoured curry) and "Tambda Rassa" (red meat flavoured curry). The examples given above simply demonstrate the diversity of food habits in India. In Kolhapur, Satara, Pune and other districts a person prefers to eat vegetables and/or curry with roti or bhaker first. Rice is served later with dal (pulses). The sequence of consuming food is culturally defined.

In fact there are cultural norms regarding what food should be prepared on certain festivals.

In India, there are norms regarding who should eat first? A general practice observation in most traditional joint families in the rural areas particularly is that men and children eat first, followed by the women folk. The Hindus in India sprinkle water clockwise around the plate, before having their meal. The Christian's world over pray and bless the food before consuming it. Well, dietary habits vary from one society to another, from one religion to another and from one region to another.

4. **Beliefs and practices regarding food to be given to an infant, a child, a pregnant woman and a new mother, a sick and a old person, a wrestler or a sports person.**

An infant is given mothers, cows, buffaloes or goats milk, for 4 to 6 months. This is followed by wearing foods popular with in a given eco-cultural system. Children are usually given light and liquid foods. In every culture these are beliefs regarding what foods should be given to a pregnant woman. Thus, hot foods leading to an abortion are avoided within 1 to 3 months of pregnancy.

Sick and elderly people are usually given light and liquid foods like porridge, smashed rice and dal, milk, curd, fruits, soup, vegetables etc. In Kolhapur, the diet of a wrestler (Pahilwan) includes, milk, dry fruits, meat, raw pulses, chicken, ghee, green leafy vegetables etc. Similarly, there are beliefs in every society, regarding what diet should a sports person be given.

5. **People's concept of food taste and satisfaction.**

Food cooked on a hearth (chulah) is believed to be very tasty. Grandmothers or mothers who prepare food is always considered to be tasty and given satisfaction. Food prepared from traditional varieties of cereals, rice, vegetables, seeds etc is believed to be tasty and gives satisfaction to people.

6. **Beliefs and practices of food quantity consumed in different seasons.**

A person from cold climate region usually eats less when he visits a hot or humid climatic region. Similarly, hot foods are consumed in less quantity in summer. People prefer cold liquids, beer, fruits, cereals, and pulses in summer.

7. **Perception regarding fasting and body maintenance.**

The belief that fasting gives rest to the digestive system, increases body vitality, contributes in body servicing and maintenance is prevalent in many societies. In fact the Hindus abstain from non-vegetarian food, liquor and other foods in the month of "Shravan". The Christains fast for 40 days during the lent period. The Muslims have strict rules regarding their fast during the Ramzan month.

Fasting is intertwined with religion and hence is strictly practiced. It revolves however on health principles. As mentioned earlier fasting gives rest to the digestive system, it cleanses the body, increases vitality of the digestive system and contributes in increasing body efficiency.

Besides this, in most societies it is observed that when a person suffers from digestive problems, he is advised to fast or take liquid food and light diet. The concept and practice of fasting is certainly associated with people's ethno-nutritional beliefs and practices.

8. **People's belief's about how food gets converted into nutrients and blood.**

Tribhuwan Robin (1998) has stated that the Thakur's believe that food gets processed in the stomach, liver and intestines and is converted into blood. The quality and colour of the blood is associated by them with strength and bodily vigour.

Further, the Thakur's also believe that blood gets converted into breast milk. Thus, if a woman consumes cold food, her blood becomes cold and further her breast milk. When her child consumes the cold milk he gets cold.

The Thakur's also believe that water, air, heat (fire element) in the human body contributes in digestion of food. Blood is the main strength of human beings. Quality of blood is directly proportional to the strength among human beings, according to the Thakur's. They believe children and youth have red blood, adults have orange blood and old people have reddish-black coloured blood. Red and orange coloured blood symbolizes vigour and strength, where as reddish-black blood symbolizes weakness and feeble aging stage of life.

Given examples regarding people's ethno-nutritional beliefs and practices regarding growth of muscles and bones.

ANALYSIS AND DISCUSSION

Primary and secondary data presented in this chapter certainly highlights people's beliefs and practices regarding body image, food, the process of digestion as viewed by people and finally the impact of certain food and nutrients on the growth and development of muscles and skeletal system.

People's rationale of the nutrient, ingredients or food that strengthens human muscles and bones depend on their perceptions and beliefs regarding the quality and characteristics present in the main source of food. For example, it is a common belief among the tribes and castes residing in remote and inaccessible areas is that monitor lizards (Ghorpads) are strong, tough, muscular and can cling on to a rock, tree or even ground persistently, hence its fat, meat and extracted oil is a source of strength. Its meat makes human muscles strong.

Table 5.2: People's Perceptions Regarding Foods that Contribute towards Growth of Muscles and Bones

Sr. No.	Community	Diet	Ethno-Nutritional Beliefs
1	2	3	4
1.	Gond Tribe of Gadchiroli District	1. Meat of chicken, peacock, green pigeon, wild boar, monitor lizard and goat 2. Green leafy vegetables such as spinich, Amaranthus, Methi; Tomatoes, Drumsticks, Gourds 3. Fruits such as Grapes and Papayas. 4. Khurmundi (Roasted and boiled head and feet of goat)	1. Contributes in making human muscles very strong. 2. Contribute in purifying blood, strengthening the human muscles and bones. 3. Strengthen the bones and joints. 4. The Gonds roast the head (mundi) and fore-legs of a goat (khur) in a fire for half an hour, clean up the hair on it and then boil it for an hour. The soup of this preparation as well as the curry is believed to strengthen bones and heal joint pairs.
2.	Mavchi Tribe of Nandurbar District	1. Boiled eggs of rural hens 2. Crabs	1. The Mavchi tribals believe that boiled eggs are patients who have fractures bones. They believe that the nutrients in the eggs contribute in joining broken bones. 2. Crab soup and curry is believed to strengthen human bones.

(Contd...)

1	2	3	4
3.	Warli Tribe of Thane District	1. Fish, Dry Fish, Crabs. 2. Rice, meat, chicken 3. Amarathus leaves	1. Soup and curry of crabs, dry fish and even fish strengthens muscles and bones of human beings. 2. Rice, meat curry and chicken contributes in growth of bones and muscles. 3. Amaranthus leaves contribute in production of quality blood.
4.	Katkaris	1. Mushroom 2. Meat of Green Pigeons	1. The Katkaris believe that certain species of mushroom that grows in the forest is a good source of strength for bones and muscles. 2. Katkaris consume green pigeon's meat for strengthening bones and muscles.
5.	Phase Pardhis	1. Peafowl and Pattridges 2. Deer Meat	1. The Phase Pardhis believe that the meat of peafowl and pattridges strengthens bones and muscles. 2. The Hareen Pardhis believe that the meat of deer makes human bones and muscles strong.

(Contd...)

1	2	3	4
6.	Madia	1. Dioscorea indica 2. Monitor Lizard 3. Red Ants	1. The Madia consume Dioscorea an underground stem for making the bones and muscles strong. 2. Meat is consumed for strengthening bones and muscles. 3. Red ants are consumed for purification of blood.

Similarly, people believe that nutrients present in the bones and flesh of rural chicken, goats, wild boar, wild pigeon, and peacock contributes in development, building, growth, joining and healing of human bones. Bone material consumed contributes construction and development of bones.

Drumstick look stiff like a bone and has a soft mass inside it, like the bone marrow in the human and animal bones and hence if consumed contributes to the growth and development of muscles and bones. The nutritional morphological and anatomical characteristics of drumsticks are co-related to human bones.

The Mavchi tribals co-relate the healthy and unhealthy quality of human bones with that of the thickness of blood that is;

- Human beings with thick blood (Jad Rakta) have strong bones.
- Those with semi-thick blood (Kami-Jad Rakta) have semi-strong bones.
- Those with thin blood (Pattal Rakta) have weak and feeble bones. People with thin blood and feeble bones reach a stage in life where they fight with disease and death, believe the Mavchi tribals.

6

Habits Life Styles Work–Culture and Low Backache

INTRODUCTION

Backache is a worldwide problem. It affects people all around the globe rich or poor alike. During the present times it has assumed a lot of significance for the reasons cited by Ebnezar John (2012:2). These reasons are as below:

1. Backache is the most common spine disorder affecting 80 per cent of the population around the globe.
2. It is next only to common cold and headache.
3. Common low – backache accounts for nearly 80 per cent of these cases (Muscular backache in 90% and facets and disc related backache in 10%).
4. Uncommon low – backache accounts for the remaining 20 per cent of the cases.
5. 8 out of the 10 people are affected with backache at some stage of life.
6. What was known as an ancient curse is now a modern international epidemic.

Causes of Low backache

Ebnezar John (2012:24 – 28) has classified two types of causes of low backache namely Direct causes (20%) and Indirect causes (Mechanical pain 80%).

(a) A quick glance at the causes of low-backaches uncommon causes of LBA: Direct Causes (20%)

Causes related to the spine: These include conditions like infection, tumors, tuberculosis, osteoporosis, spondylsis, fracture etc.

Problems not related to the spine: These include problems in other systems like genitourinary tract, gastro – intestinal tract, prolapsed of the uterus, chronic white discharge in females etc.

(b) Common causes of LBA: Indirect Causes (Mechanical Back Pain – 80%)

These account for 8 out of 10 cases. The common varieties of low backache are muscular strains, ligament sprains and disc disease. The causes for these maladies are:

1. Repeated physical and mental stress.
2. Poor postural habits.
3. Improper lifting of weights.
4. Mental depression.
5. Unaccustomed activities.
6. Improper work culture and work habits.

Objectives

The present chapter aims at understanding the social, physical, cultural and medical aspects of low-backache, keeping in view the following objectives:

1. To study the prevalence and causes of low-backache.
2. To explore the impact of habits, life styles and work culture on low-backache among different occupational and cultural groups.
3. To document people's perception about origin and cause of low – backache.

RESEARCH METHODOLOGY

This chapter is based on analysis of secondary and primary data on the socio-cultural and work culture habits associated with low-backache. The authors have reviewed relevant literature related to the research problem. Besides this focused group discussions were held with male and female members of Warli, Thakur and Gond tribes of Maharashtra.

FINDINGS

Based on the analysis of secondary and primary data, the findings of this chapter are presented as below:

1. Walking, sitting, standing and sleeping habits and backache.

(a) Walking habit and its impact on Lower back

Orthopaedic surgeons and physiotherapists advice people to walk straight and on even ground. They recommend the use of quality, branded and good sports or walking shoes, to avoid stress on the spine, which goes up many times during improper walking. This further rises as one climbs, jumps and runs.

Use of high-heel shoes, sandals or footwear, especially among females who are office executives, secretaries, models, teachers, actors etc is very common. Their lifestyle, occupational dress code and status demands wearing of high-heel shoes, sandals or foot wear on various occasions. Wearing of this causes backache, because walking with fancy or high-heeled foot wear usually take short steps, wide steps, oblique steps etc. Her shoulder and chest may be drooping exclusively on one side; she may be carrying unequal loads on her shoulder, head or back. She soon realizes that her spine has gone up many times during the improper walking.

In doing so, she knowingly or unknowingly insults her spine and fails to maintain the nature recommended s-curve of the spine. In this process the spine battles many fold to overcome the ill effects of the poor posture and style of walking. Well, given above is just one example of lifestyle, economic status, class, use of high-heels and walking styles and its impact on spine.

The table given below shows various occupational groups who maintain a faulty walking posture while at work place, for one to three hours per day.

Table 6.1: Table Showing Work Culture and Walking Habits/Postures in Selected Occupational Groups

Sr. No.	Occupation Group	Walking Posture While Working
1	2	3
1.	Coolies who load and unload grain bags	Coolies, who load and unload grain bags weighing 100kg, carry them on backs and walk up to the place of unloading. Their body posture is such that the weight is on their back; they bend and move forward walking slowly towards the unloading point. Their poor socio-economic status and occupation demands this type of walking posture while carrying the load on their back.
2.	Agricultural Labourers	Agricultural labourers, both males and females bend down while, transplanting rice, weeding and harvesting. They too walk while in bending posture. They have to do this for earning their daily wage and for livelihood.
3.	Sugarcane Cutters	In Maharashtra there are 7, 50,000 sugarcane cutters, out of 2, 50,000 are children (Panjiar Smita: 2007). These sugarcane cutters are given a target to cut at least one truck full of sugarcane and load it. While cutting they bend and cut sugarcane and slowly walk. This process of work imposes stress on their spine.

(Contd...)

1	2	3
4.	Coolies at the Railway Station and Bus Stops	Coolies at the railway stations and bus stops walk with heavy loads on their heads. These heavy loads certainly have impact on their cervical region and the spine. However, they do this, because their occupation demands it.
5.	Rag Pickers	The rag pickers in the cities and towns, who hail mostly from slums, have to bend don and walk and bend to pick up rags several times during the day.
6.	Stone Quarry Workers	In their book captioned, "Stone Quarry Workers.(2008) have revealed that both men and women suffer from low backache, because they carry stones on their heads and walk for some distance to unload the same.
7.	Fuel Wood Sellers	Most women in tribal areas go to the forest walking at least 3-8 kms. They cut fuel wood and make bundles to take them home either for household use or to sell in the local market. These women walk with the head load of fuel wood for 3-8 kms to the local market. It is a walk for 1.5 to 2 hours. This work culture does have an impact on their spine.
8.	Washer man	Washer man, belonging to "Dhobi", "Warti" or "Parit" caste who are into the business of washing and ironing clothes have to constantly be in a bending position when they wash clothes. The move in a slightly bent posture when they carry the washed to dry them on ropes. Secondly, while ironing the clothes they have to bend forward many times. Carrying the load of washed and ironed clothes to their clients on the head and walking is difficult a task. These washer men and their wives often suffer from low-backache problems.

Well, one can go on quoting examples of occupational groups from the informal sectors, who have no choice, but to carry heavy loads and walk in a bent posture while working. Thus, occupation and backache is closely intertwined and varies too from one occupational group to another.

There is an urgent need to create awareness among people regarding the technique of walking. The technique should be such that your back is stressed very little while you propel yourself forward over your feet. Ebnezar John (2012:70) provides a key to practicing the right walking principles, mentioned below:

1. Head should be held high.
2. The chin should be tucked in.
3. Toes should point straight.
4. Wear comfortable footwear.
5. Do not wear high heels.

(b) Sitting habit and its impact on Lower Back

As aptly pointed out by Ebnezar John (2012:35) that, sitting is one of the most stressful events on ones spine. Mere sitting increases the stress on your spine, he says. He further adds that, 60 per cent of our lifetime is spent in sitting.

People sit awkwardly in a chair with their backs hunched over computers, reading tables, dining tables, conferences etc. Some people sit on a stool with no back support. Most sofas, chairs, benches and stools people sit on are imperfectly designed. When people commute to their offices in public transport systems like buses, autos, local trains and taxis where they seldom get to sit on scientifically designed chairs. Some people use two wheelers to go to their offices, schools and colleges.

Life in the cities is too hectic and brings its own pressure situations which your spine would well have liked to dispense with. Due to long distances one has to leave home quite early, this means little time for morning exercises. Poor public transport systems, bad roads, overcrowded trains and buses etc forces people to rely mainly on their own modes of transportation mostly two wheelers. Ebnezar John an eminent orthopaedic expert states that two wheelers are extremely hazardous for back.

2. Sitting habits, work culture and socio-economic status

Medical science has its own scientific interpretation about how ones sitting posture should be, however it does not take into account people's ignorance, awareness, lack of scientific knowledge about sitting postures. Sitting postures and habits are very closely intertwined with people's socio-economic status and work culture. For example students in most rural and tribal areas still sit on the floor without chairs, desks and tables. Most hawkers, vegetable and fruit vendors in rural, tribal and even urban areas sit in one posture without a chair for hours in their respective open air markets. Middle and lower class people, who cannot afford to buy cars, travel by mobikes and bicycles. We come across several people who travel by bullock-carts, tractors, trucks, jeeps in crowded conditions. Peons, sweepers and drivers in most offices do not have a stool to sit on. Sitting arrangement varies from one working environment to other.

While discussing about how our backs are abused at the places of work, Ebnezar John (2012: 41-45) revealed four types of social and economic classes whose sitting posture and work environment varied.

These working classes are:

(a) The Upper Group

(b) The Middle Group

(c) The Lower Group

(d) The Special Group (Professional Group)

(a) The Upper Group

According to Ebnezar John (2012), this group includes the white collared professionals like bureaucrats, politicians, managers, secretaries and top executives. They are an enlisted class and work in cozy atmosphere like A.C rooms, with T.V, computers, fax etc. They sit on ill-designed chairs for hours without any intervening breaks, moreover the posture they adopt in these chairs are far from satisfactory. They hunch their backs over their working tables and may even sit up with their legs stretched on the table piping cigars. They suffer from enormous work pressure leading to depression. Their busy schedule leaves them with particularly no time for quality exercises, which can tone up their back muscles. The net result of all this is pressure, pressure and more pressure on the spine. Backache thus becomes an inescapable part of their lives.

(b) The Middle Group

If this is the story of the elite group, now consider the story of the middle group. Their tales are different but the end result is the same. This group states Ebnezar John (2012) is a very large working class as they form a major part of the working force in any organisation. The clerks, secretaries, assistants, typists, stenographers, computer engineers etc come under this group. They work under lots of stress. Most of them work for 8-10 hours.

In her study on the life styles of IT personnel in Pune city, Khatare Akrami (2012) has revealed following facts about the IT professionals she researched on:

1. That, over 70 per cent work for more than 10 hours in front of a computer screen.
2. That, most of them suffer from low backache.
3. That, several IT computer professionals do not maintain food and sleeping timings.
4. That, most of them suffer from work load and target stress.

Sitting in the office for long hours and even on holidays is a common feature among the clerks, assistants, desk officers and stenographers of some Government Departments. The above mentioned staff especially in the Integrated Tribal Development Department, where in target completion is a must, sit for long hours on the chairs to achieve their targets. In this process, they suffer from problems such as piles and of course backache.

Ebnezar John (2012) states, that this class of workers sit on everything except for chairs which are economically designed specifically for the back. Moreover, about the posture they adopt in these chairs, the less said the better. They work under extreme physical and mental stress and most of the times have poor working facilities. The babus of Vidarbha region in Maharashtra work under extreme hot conditions from March to June every summer. The situation becomes worse when there is no electricity. There is no escaping backache for this group as well.

(c) The Lower Group

To these belong the peons, attenders, office boys, watchman, security guards, cleaners, gardeners, scavengers etc, according to Ebnezar John (2012). He further states that in this group, their back is subjected to a different kind of pressure but not from sitting but standing for long hours. They have to do lots of mundane jobs like lifting weights, carrying things around, guarding the doors, cleaning etc. They also work under extreme stress and their working environment is far from being ideal. Result is backache at some or the other stage of life. Ebnezar John (2012) also includes people like construction workers, porters, loaders, agriculture workers, coolies etc.

(d) Special Groups

High Backache Risk Professions

1. Doctors, especially surgeons' stand for a long time in one position while operating or treating a patient. So are the nurses and paramedical workers.
2. The work of traffic policemen, soldiers, security guards etc require them to stand for longer periods under the deafening noise of the traffic and bullets.
3. Computer engineers and other software professionals sit unknowingly in improper chairs that too in improper posture for a long period. Increased pressure of work and stress further complicates the matter.
4. The other professions, which is very unkind for back is that of judiciary. Judges need to sit for a long period of time from 10am to 5pm with only one-hour lunch break

in between. Similarly, the lawyers need to stand for a long time to argue their cases.

5. Sports persons and athletes are also prone for back injuries from minor sprains to major fractures and dislocation of the spine.

All these special group of professionals are very much prone to suffer from severe backache in the later stages of life. Thus, backache makes no distinction between a bureaucrat and an ordinary labourer or professional, and strikes with impurity people belonging to all religions, castes, races, creed, professions and countries. (Ebnezar John 2012)

Dr. John Ebnezar has given examples of bad sitting and correct sitting. These are as below:

(i) **Examples of Bad Sitting**

- **Slumping:** Here the tail bone is bent under you, your low back bends outwards and the upper back is rounded forwards. This happens when you slump in your chairs while sitting. A very common unhealthy back practice.
- **Uptight Sitting:** This causes low level tightening of muscles and you need to hold the spine erect without support.
- **Sitting Still:** Sitting still for too long in the same position creates negative forces, which reduces the sitting tolerance even further.

(ii) **Examples of Correct Sitting**

Dr. John Ebnezar (2012) recommends the right posture of sitting which is as below:

- Neck should be slightly forward and upper back is straight.
- Shoulders must be released and the arms must hang naturally.
- Back must be in full contact with the back rest.
- Angle behind the knees and the angle of your back with the sit must be greater than 90°, this decreases the pressure on the spine, abdomen and legs.

- Elbows and hands must rest comfortably on the arms of the chair.
- Thighs must be parallel to the floor and feet must be flat.

3. Standing habits and its impact on back

Standing in one position for long, especially with high heels and improper footwear. Standing with the shoulders drooping, chest sunk in or your knees tucked up. Ebnezar John (2012:35) states that mere standing the stress, which was least on the spine in lying position, increases three times. This stress increases manifold when a person stands incorrectly.

It is pertinent to note that there are several occupational groups in the informal sector, that are required to stand for long time, while at work. These occupational groups are:

1. Watchmen, security guards, peons, soldiers.
2. Hawkers, vegetable sellers, construction workers.
3. Traffic police, police.
4. Surgeons, nurses, professors etc.

These occupational groups suffer from backache.

4. Sleeping habits and its impact on back

Sleeping though least stressful to ones back, still needs care. An average individual sleeps for at least six to eight hours a day. When so much time is spent sleeping it's logical that our posture while sleeping has to be right and so is the choice of bed. (Ebnezar John: 72)

Choice of beds, mattresses, pillows, cots, and sleeping environment is closely connected with socio-economic status of a family. In their book captioned, "Streets of Insecurity: A Study of Pavement Dwellers", Tribhuwan Robin and Ragnahild (2004) have revealed that the permanent pavement dwellers sleep on the streets without cots, beds, mattresses and pillows. They use bed sheets, cardboards, flex hoardings, old saris, and news papers to sleep on the floor. Choosing cozy bed, bed cover mattress is a dream to this class of people. Similarly, studies by Tribhuwan Robin, 2004, 1996, 1998, 2004 have revealed that most tribals do not use good mattresses, bed covers, and pillows as they cannot afford them.

Those belonging to the upper class use soft and cozy mattresses and pillows, but many of them are unaware of the correct sleeping postures. Sleeping on stomachs is a common feature of people who use soft beds and pillows. Whether rich or poor, there is an urgent need to create awareness about correct sleeping habits.

5. Socio-economic status and backache

(a) Can the coolies, who lift grain bags on their back, afford to give up their occupation to save their backs?

(b) Can they afford to purchase good quality beds, mattresses, bed covers, and pillows to save their backs?

(c) Can they afford to purchase ergonomic chairs?

(d) Are they aware of the scientific and right postures of sitting, sleeping and standing?

(e) Do these questions apply to the several occupational groups in the informal or unorganized sector?

Well, these and several others questions haunt the mind of a social scientist and more precisely medical Anthropologists, who study health, disease, treatment, health expenditure pattern, health seeking behaviour etc from a holistic perspective. There is a need to find out theoretical and practical solutions to the above research questions that debate over socio-economic status and musculo-skeletal disorders.

The authors of this book, have discussed the issue of the economics of orthopaedic treatment in a separate chapter in detail, showing the significance of social, economic and educational status and health expenditure behaviour, with reference to orthopaedic disorders.

7

Rheumatoid Arthritis of the Hands and Feet *People's Perception*

WHAT IS ARTHRITIS ?

Arthritis is a non specific term denoting acute or chronic inflammation of the joints. It is characterized by pain, swelling and limitation of joint movements.

Arthritis are classified on the basis of number of joints involved.

Monoarthritis: when only one joints are involved.

Oligoarthritis : when 2 to 5 joints are involved.

Polyarthritis : when more than 5 joints are involved.

TYPES OF ARTHRITIS

- Osteoarthritis
- Rhematoid arthritis
- Infective arthritis
- Metabolic arthritis
- Neuropathic joint disorder
- Haemophilic arthritis
- Psoriatic arthritis

- Psycogenic arthritis
- Ankylosing spondylitis

According to orthopaedic experts there are various types of arthritis affecting the young and elderly people but the most common arthritis which are seen in day to day life are as follows:

- Osteoarthritis
- Rhematoid arthritis
- Infective arthritis
- Ankylosing spondylitis

This chapter throws light on the medical and socio-cultural beliefs regarding rheumatoid arthritis and more particularly about the rheumatoid arthritis of hands and feet. Before getting into cultural belief and practises regarding rheumatoid arthritis of hands and feet let us try to understand what rheumatoid arthritis is.

WHAT IS RHEUMATOID ARTHRITIS ?

Rheumatoid arthritis is a chronic inflammatory autoimmune disease in which there is a inflammation of synovial tissue in the peripheral joints leads to joint erosion and destructions of joints

John Ebnezar (2000:338) has stated that Rheumatoid arthritis is the most common inflammatory disease of the joints. It is a systemic disease of young and middle aged adults characterized by destruction of the joint. Eventually joints are destroyed, fibrosed or ankylosed.

About Rheumatoid arthritis It is said that "It bite the joints, licks all other system of the body and barks at the treating physician".

Admas J.C and Hamblen (2001:116) have defined rheumatoid arthritis as a chronic inflammation of joints often associated with mild constitutional symptoms. It nearly always affect several joints at same time.

Rheumatoid arthritis is a auto immune disorder of unknown aetiology and characterized by destruction of joint, deformity, disability and premature death. It affects the smaller joints of hands and feet, although any synovial joint may be affected.

PREVALENCE OF RHEUMATOID ARTHRITIS

The disease is more common in females. The female male ratio is 4:1 Prevalance in adult varies from 0.5 per cent to 3.8 per cent. Peak age of onset is in fourth decades in females and slightly later in males. In 80 per cent of the patients disease is seen between the ages of 35-50 years. 40-60 per cent of patient with advanced rheumatoid arthritis dies earlier than their expected life span.

CLINICAL FEATURES

Rheumatoid Arthritis is characterised by joint pain, stiffness and symmetrical swelling of peripheral joints of hands and feet.

Initially pain may be experienced only on movement of joints but rest pain and prolonged early morning stiffness occurs gradually and are characterised features of rheumatoid arthritis Rheumatoid arthritis is a chronic polyarthritis. Patient also gives history of weight loss, lethargy, general weakness, anorexia, depression etc.

In typical cases smaller joints of the fingers and toes are first to be affected. As the disease progresses, it spreads to involve the wrist, elbow, shoulder, knees and ankles. The hip joints involved only in more severely affected cases.

RECENT (REVISED) CRITERIA FOR RHEUMATOID ARTHRITIS (1987)

According to the American college of rheumatology, at least 4 out of 7 criteria given below should be fulfilled by patient to make a diagnosis of rheumatoid arthritis.

(a) Morning stiffness around the joints for an hour or more.
(b) Arthritis of three or more joints (swelling) more than six weeks.
(c) Arthritis of hand joints (swelling) for more than six weeks.
(d) Symmetrical arthritis or symmetrical swelling for more than six weeks.

(e) Rheumatoid nodules.
(f) Rheumatoid factors (serum)
(g) Radiographic changes.

DEFORMITIES IN RHEUMATOID ARTHRITIS

Most common deformities seen in Rheumatoid arthritis are:

1. "Swan neck deformity" of fingers of hands.
2. Boutonniere or button – hole deformity of fingers of hands.
3. 'Z' deformity of Thumb
4. Trigger fingers and trigger thumb.
5. Clawing of toes.
6. Hammer toe.

HOW RHEUMATOID ARTHRITIS IS DIAGNOSED ?

It is diagnosed on the basis of signs and symptoms, (clinical features) of the patients, physical examination, X-rays, blood test etc.

TREATMENT

According to orthopaedic literature, the treatment of rheumatoid arthritis is not satisfactory. No specific cure has been found. Adams and Hamblen (2001:120) have classified methods of treatment of the disease which is as follows.

1. Rest and constitutional Treatment
2. Drug – therapy

   Drugs are used regularly.
   - Analgesics.
   - Anti-inflamatory Drugs
   - Disease modifying drugs.
   - Steroids.
3. Intra-articular injection of hydro cortisone.
4. Physiotherapy.
5. Occupational therapy.
6. Surgery

Well, given above is the scientific, medical or allopathic interpretation of the rheumatoid arthritis of hands and feet.

This chapters unveils people's perception regarding the origin and cause, its classification, the treatment and other beliefs and practises associated with the rheumatoid arthritis of hands and feet only.

Research Methodology

The present study was carried out in the general hospital, Gadchiroli, in the state of Maharashtra, India. The researchers interviewed 50 outdoor patients with rheumatoid arthritis from January to December, 2012.

Interview schedule was prepared to study the perception of the rural respondents regarding the origin, cause & treatment of rheumatoid arthritis. statistical data was entered in excel so as to prepare & interpret relevant tables. Qualitative data was analyzed manually.

Major Findings of the Study

1. Out of the total 50 respondent all the 50 suffered from rheumatoid arthritis of the wrist and the phalanges.
2. **Awareness Regarding the disease.**

   100 per cent of the respondents were unaware that their disease was known by the name rheumatoid arthritis.
3. **Local name**

   All of them said that the desire is locally known as "wat," except one bengali patient, who is living in Gadchiroli for over 60 years pronounced it as "Bat".
4. **Origin & cause of the disease.**

   It was observed that 73 per cent of the respondents said that the disease is caused due to lack of pure blood to the wrist fingers of the hand and due to damaged veins, arteries & nerves. 11 per cent said it is caused due to exposure of hands to cold water & air. 6 per cent said it is caused because their blood turned into blackish colure. 2 per cent said it is caused due to "Karma" (deeds). 3 per cent stated it is caused due to cold blood getting into wrist & finger joints. 4 per cent said it is caused due to weak bones, while 1 per cent did not respond.

5. **Concept of massage.**

   It was observed that all the respondent tried massage therapy, with the help of their spouse, children, a masseur or by themselves. the oils used for massage were "sarso" (Brassica junea), "Mauha" (Madhuca indica) and "khobra" – coconut (Cocos nucifera).

   The patients opined that massage contributes in relaxing the nerves, veins & arteries. They said, "Malish mule shira mokdya hotat."Some felt that the medical oil gets into the bones. Massage helps in the movement of the bones, there by reducing the stiffens of the bone.

6. **Hydo-Therapy**

   About 20 per cent of the respondent opined that washing their fingers & wrist in hot water relieves pain.

7. **Diet therapy**

   Over 50 per cent of the respondent said that meat of country (local)chicken, bones of goats, eggs, tomato's, beetroot, green vegetable are a good therapy for "wat".

8. **When do they go to an allopath ?**

   Almost all the respondent stated that they consulted an orthopedic doctor in the general hospital when they are in severe pain.

9. **Expenditure pattern**

   Out of the total number of respondents interviewed it was observed that 49 per cent spend Rs. 500 to 2000/-; 31 per cent Rs 2001 to 3000/-, and 15 per cent spend above 3000/-, on their treatment & diet while 5 per cent did not respond.

Case Study No. 1

Mr. RM, aged 67, a married male, with two sons & two daughters, from Netaji nagar, of Goth village, Chamorshi tehsil, in Gadchiroli district, in the state of Maharashtra India. It is a migrant from west Bangal.

History of the Disease

Mr. RM said, that he became a victim of rheumatoid arthritis at the age of 60. The bones of the fingers of both the hands were protruding out showing an extra growth. This condition is called batronial deformity. This wrist was slightly crooked. These joints are painful he said. On enquiring whether any one in the family had this disease, his response was no.

Origin and Cause

According Mr. RM, the baronial deformity of the fingers and crooked nose of the wrist was caused due to rapturing of nerves of the wrists and fingers he called thickness of the bones or batonial deformity as "gath".

Problems Faced

As a result of the advance stage of rheumatoid arthritis of hands as well as feet, including the hip joints, Mr. RM said, he can not sit properly; her squat not can get up easily. He is in a lying position most of the time.

Social Problems

He said my relatives, friends and community folks do not touch me & are scared to shake hands with me. I am unable to attend religious rituals & function. My family members do not take me for social & cultural gathering and function like wedding, Durga puja etc.

My son & his wife give me food twice a day, because the house is on my name. My grandchildren, do not play nor talk to me. This disease has out casted me out of my family & community.

Money Spent on Treatment

Mr. R.M said that, thus far he has spent over Rs. 5000/- on treatment & consultation of the disease, but he has not been cured of it. Infact it is becoming worse day by day.

Analysis

An advance stage of rheumatoid arthritis can not only cause physical problems for a patient, but mental and social problems as well.

Case study No. 2

Mrs. S, aged 48, a married female, from Saoli, tehsil, district Chandrapur, Suffered from rheumatoid arthritis, since the age of 38.

History of the Disease

Mrs. S is the only person in her family, who has the disease. She does not know that it is called rheumatoid arthritis. The local name for the disorder is known as "wat". she said.

Origin and Cause

According to Mrs. S, the disease is caused due to exposure of hands to cold water & air. She said that as a house wife, she has to get up in the morning fetch drinking water, wash vessels & clothes, cook food' work in the field & go to fetch fuel wood. Exposure of her hands to cold water & air resulted into rheumatoid arthritis.

Problems Faced

She has not faced any social problems, due to the disease. Her husband & relatives understand her. However, she finds it difficult to pick up heavy objects. There is sever pain in the joints some times.

Money Spent on the Disease

Mrs. S must have spent about Rs. 3000/- on the treatment of the disorder, thus far.

Analysis

Female patients who are burdened with household & agriculture responsibility are over worked & hena feel that exposure of their hands to cold water & air leads to rheumatoid arthritis.

Concluding Remarks

Although rheumatoid arthritis is a medically interpreted physical problem it cross-cuts social, cultured & psychological spheres of human life. people in the tribal and rural areas are unaware of the scientific aspects of rheumatoid arthritis and its different forms. Efforts must he made to create awareness among people to prevent the disorder.

8

Osteoporosis
Socio-cultural Beliefs and Practices Among the Gonds and Thakurs of Maharashtra, India

–Dr. J.C. Kurian
–Dr. Robin D. Tribhuwan
–Dr. Satish Meshram

INTRODUCTION

Orthopedic surgeons today are concerned with diseases and injuries to the bones, joints, trunk and limbs. Their field includes the study of the nerves and blood vessels too. Adams & Hamblem (2001). In fact, the medical field of orthopedics is so vast, that an orthopedic surgeon takes years and decades of practice before he is considered a specialist by others in his field. There are several diseases of the limbs, trunk, joints, and bones and the skeletal system in general. It is difficult for a layman to understand these disorders and the scientific etiology associated with them. However, the concept of disease and its etiology varies from one society to another.

From time immemorial diseases, ailments, conditions, pain and suffering have been problems of every society and as such, every known society in the world have developed methods of coping with this universal problem by creating their own system of medicine Caudil (1955). Newell (1975) has rightly stated that, throughout the ages, man has been devising ways and means of caring for the sick in their community.

As aptly pointed out by Tribhuwan and Gambhir (1995), every culture, has its own beliefs and practices regarding health and diseases. It is to such beliefs and practices regarding health and disease, which are products of indigenous cultural development and not explicitly derived from the conceptual frame work of modern medicine, that the term "Ethno medicine" is applied. Hughes (1968)

Thus, even before the advent of modern medicine, traditional folk, the world over, had developed culture specific beliefs and practices regarding health and disease. This paper unveils the socio-cultural beliefs and practices regarding osteoporosis among the Gonds and Thukur Tribals of Maharashtra State in India. It is based on empirical enquiry into the ethno medical systems of two tribes. Its prime concern is to show, what tribals perceive, believe and practice about an orthopedic disorder such as osteoporosis, keeping in view the following objectives.

OBJECTIVES OF THE PAPER

1. To present the scientific and medical interpretation of osteoporosis.
2. To understand the tribal perceptions of growth and development of the human bones.
3. To unveil the beliefs and practices associated with osteoporosis among the Gonds and Thakurs.
4. To recommend strategies to create awareness among tribals about osteoporosis.

RESEARCH METHODOLOGY

The present field work was carried out among two major tribes of Maharashtra, namely the Gonds of Gadchiroli and Thakurs of Raigad districts respectively. The Gond informants were drawn from two villages of Armori block of Gadchiroli district namely Thane gaon and Wadaha gaon. The Thakur respondents were selected from Nagewadi and Khondyachi wadi, two hamlets of the Pathraj village in the Karjat block of Raigad district.

Research Tools and Data Collection

Data was collected and recorded using anthropological tools and techniques. In-depth interviews of key informants from both the tribes, such as patients, family and village elders and the ethno medical specialists were carefully registered. Participant observation was carried out by participating in rituals of diagnosis, healing and thanks giving. Thus, qualitative data was gathered by interviewing 50 Thakurs and 50 Gonds. Besides this, in-depth interviews of 5 bone setters, 5 herbalists and 5 midwives were collected from the Gonds as well as the Thakurs respectively. The data was analyzed manually as it was qualitative in nature.

WHAT IS OSTEOPOROSIS ?

Osteoporosis is a common disease of the bone characterized by decreased bone mass and bone strength. Loss of bone mass makes the bone porous, fragile and hence more vulnerable to fractures especially at the spine, hip and wrist.

In many affected people, bone loss is gradual and without any indications, or warning signs until the disease has advanced. Osteoporosis is also known as "the silent killer" because a person usually doesn't know they have the problem until it's too late.

According to Surya (1993), osteoporosis is by far the commonest metabolic bone disease. It is characterized by a diffuse reduction in the bone density due to decrease in the bone mass.

Adams & Hamblen (2001), Maheshwari (1993) and Surya (1993) have outlined the causes of osteoporosis which is given below:

- Low Bone mass Density (also known as bone mineral density).

  Example – Men have higher density than women. Women are at more risk of osteoporosis than men.
- Several etiological factors may be operative in a given patient. The commonest factor in males is senility and in females it is menopause.

- Protein deficiency
- Post menopausal conditions
- Post immobilization as in bed–ridden patients.
- Life style factors
- Genetic factors
- Old Age
- Lone term steroid therapy
- Mal–absorption of minerals

Osteoporosis in Asia - Tentative Statistics

Country or Region	*Extrapolated Prevalence	**Population in 2011
Bangladesh	14,549,755	142,319,000
Bhutan	224,985	720,679
China	133,704,906	1,347,350,000
Timor-Leste	104,923	1,066,409
Hong Kong	705,674	7,103,700
India	109,639,624	1,210,193,422
Indonesia	24,546,628	237,641,326
Japan	13,107,809	127,610,000
Laos	624,659	6,465,800
Macau	45,838	557,400
Malaysia	2,421,432	28,334,135
Mongolia	283,223	2,844,000
Philippines	8,877,821	92,337,852
Papua New Guinea	557,970	6,469,000
Vietnam	8,509,406	87,840,000
Singapore	448,194	5,183,700
Pakistan	16,387,858	179,709,000
North Korea	2,336,512	24,051,218
South Korea	4,965,240	48,580,000
Sri Lanka	2,049,061	20,883,000
Taiwan	2,341,895	23,245,018
Thailand	6,677,333	65,479,453

* www.cureresearch.com/o/osteoporosis/stats-country_printer.htm

** en.wikipedia.org/wiki/List_of_countries_by_population

There are many ailments or conditions in Western industrialized societies today that were unheard of, or at least very rare, just a century ago. The same conditions are still unheard of among non-literate peoples who do not have the 'benefits' of the advancement of science and the knowledge we have today. Many scholars tell us that there is a very good reason for this: They eat what Nature intended; we don't. Hippocrates, the father of modern medicine says, "Let food be thy medicine and medicine be thy food."

Dr. Love (1997) says, Central American Indian women, for example, live for an average of thirty years after the menopause but they don't get osteoporosis, they don't lose height, they don't develop a dowager's hump and they don't get fractures. A research team analyzed their hormone levels and bone density and found that their estrogen levels were no higher than those of white American women — in some cases they were even lower. Bone density tests by a research team showed that bone loss occurred in these women at the same rate as their US counterparts. So why didn't they suffer fractures?

Drs. Dawson-Hughes and Harris (2002), of the Calcium and Bone Metabolism Laboratory, Tufts University, Boston, Massachusetts, USA, tested associations between protein intake and change in bone mass density in 342 healthy men and women aged 65 or over who had completed a 3-year, randomized, placebo-controlled trial of calcium and vitamin D supplementation. They found that higher protein intake was significantly associated with a favorable 3-year change in total-body bone mass density in the supplemented group but not in the placebo group.

In Papua New Guinea along with plant medicines and traditional therapies for treating physical symptoms, patients and caregivers use rituals designed to overcome or ascertain the causes of sickness and mental illness, such as ruptured social relations, sorcerers, and ghost attacks. In many areas, women and girls are fed significantly less than men and boys, resulting in weight loss, anemia, osteoporosis, and greater susceptibility to illness.

Signs and Symptoms

Orthopedic experts have revealed that osteoporosis conditions can operate silently for decades because the disease doesn't cause symptoms until a bone fracture occurs. In the early stages of bone loss, one usually has no pain or symptoms. But, once weakened by osteoporosis, some of the signs and symptoms are as follows:

- Back pain
- Loss of height
- Stooped posture
- Fracture of the vertebrae, wrists, hip and/or other bones.
- Pain in the neck region
- Pain in the thoracic or chest cavity
- Loss of Tooth

Significant Facts about Osteoporosis

- 80 per cent of those affected by osteoporosis are women.
- 1 out of 3 women and 1 out of 8 men over the age of 50 will have an osteoporosis–related fracture in their life time.
- Significant risk has been reported in people of all ethnic backgrounds.
- Osteoporosis can strike at any age.

Risk Factors

Orthopedic experts have revealed a number of factors that can increase the likelihood that will develop osteoporosis which includes:

1. **Family history:** Osteoporosis runs in families. For that reason, having a parent or sibling with the disease, puts you at greater risk, especially if you also have a family history of fractures.
2. **Frame size:** Men and women who have these and small body frames tend to have higher risk because they have less bone mass to draw from as they age.
3. **Tobacco use:** According to research scholars, the use of tobacco contributes to weak bones.

4. **Estrogen deficiency:** Deficiency of estrogen (female sex hormone) as seen after menopause and surgical removal of the ovaries.
5. **Eating disorders:** Eating disorders such as anorexia nervosa and bulimia can cause osteoporosis.
6. **Medications:** Long term use of certain medication like corticosteroids, diuretics and blood–thinning medications can cause bone loss.
7. **Breast Cancer:** Post menopausal women who have had breast cancer are at increased risk of osteoporosis, especially if they were treated with chemotherapy.
8. **Low Calcium intake:** A life long lack of calcium plays a major role in the development of osteoporosis. Low calcium intake, especially before 30 years of age, contributes to poor bone density, early loss of bone and an increased risk of fractures.

Given, the above allopathic interpretation of osteoporosis let us look into the tribal perception of the disease, its signs, symptoms, causes, preventive and curative precautions as viewed by them from an insider's (emic) perspective.

OSTEOPOROSIS: TRIBAL PERCEPTION

In depth interviews with patients, elderly people, bone setters, mid wives and herbalists reveal that both the Gonds and the Thakurs have no clear cut name for the disease, Osteoporosis. The Thakurs refer to the disease to a condition of deteriorating or degeneration of bones. The traditional name for the condition is "hadya zijane" The Gonds on the other hand refer the condition to weakening of bones after 45 years of age.

Some of the signs and symptoms of the disease as perceived by the Gonds and Thakurs are as follows:

1. Blood of such people become redish black. It does not have strength (takat).
2. Bones become soft like cotton or wet coconut fiber.
3. People with this condition have less flesh.

4. They complain of joint, muscle, bone and back pain.
5. They eat less.
6. Women who have heavy work load become victims of the disease.
7. They do not work nor walk around in the village.

Etiology of Osteoporosis

Some of the etiological explanations of the Thakurs and Gond patients studied, are as follows:

- Wrath of gods and goddesses
- Witch craft and sorcery
- Bad luck
- Breach of cultural taboo
- Poor growth and development of bones.

Therapy

What comes spiritually must be healed spiritually and hence the role of shamans, bone setters, herbalists and midwives becomes crucial. Studies by Harner (1973), Schutlur (1976), Lieban (1973), Foster and Anderson (1983), Kurian & Tribhuwan (1990), Tribhuwan & Gambhir (1995), Jain & Tribhuwan (1996), Tribhuwan (1998), have revealed that tribal medical specialists are looked upon with respect by their community members for their medical skills, knowledge and surely for the health services they render.

Depending on the cause perceived the medical practitioner provides a therapy. He or she may combine herbal, mechanical and magico-religious therapies or use one as the case may be some of the major therapies are as below:

1. Appeasing the pathogenic agents by offering a chicken sacrifice, a Coconut (*Cocos nucifera)*, "Mauha" liquor *(Bassia latifolia)* or at times sacrificing a goat.
2. Recommending massage of "Mauha" seed oil, Mustard or "Sarso" oil *(Brassica juncea)* or "Ghorpad" or monitor lizard (*Varanus sp.)* oil.
3. Recommending the patients to take chicken, meat and wild boar soup, chewing soft bones and non-vegetarian diet is yet another recommendation.

4. Recommend consumption of "Ghorpad" or monitor lizard (*Varanus sp.)* meat and body massage with the oil prepared from the fat of the monitor lizard.
5. Consumptions of vegetables such as Spinach or "Palak" (*Spinacia oleracea*), "Chavli Bhajee" (*Amaranthus spinosus*), Tomatoes (*Lycopersicon esculentum*), Bottle-gourd or "Dudhi Bhopala" (*Lagenaria siceraria*), Drum stick (*Moringa oleifera*), Fenugreek or Methi (*Trigonella foenum-graecum*) which gives strength to the bones.
6. Consumptions of meat of green pigeon strengthen the bones.
7. Consumption of Papaya (*Carica papaya*) is believed to reduce pain of the joints, bones as well backache.
8. The Gond bone setters recommend the consumption of boiled hooves and head of goats. They believe that by doing so the bones become strong.
9. The elderly folk of both the tribes stated that the powder of Babul seeds (*Acacia nilotica*) should be taken with milk or water and the decoction would make the muscles strong and flexible.
10. The Thakur bone setters, herbalists, Shamans and midwives recommend consumption of Nachni porridge (*Eleucine coracana*). They believe it makes the muscles and bones strong as well as strengthens blood.

Interestingly among Thakurs as well as Gonds milk and milk products are not consumed. In fact they do not milk their cows. They believe by milking the cows, the young calves are deprived of milk. Both tribes consume tea without milk. Scientifically speaking, milk is rich in calcium and proteins and this could have saved many of the tribal folk from Osteoporosis. It was also observed that the first milk of the weaning mother containing colostrums (which builds immunity in babies) was not given to the new born in both the tribal communities. They believe it is spoilt (Naska) milk. Instead, the new born was given honey or brown sugar water for two days.

The Gonds as well as Thakurs believe that for nine months and nine days during pregnancy a woman does not menstruate. This spoilt (menstrual) blood which does not come out of the body, mixes with her normal blood. Breast milk is produced from a woman's blood. Blood gets converted into milk. Now, the menstrual as well as the normal blood gets converted into thick milk, that is colostrum (Naska dudh) and hence it is not given to the new born. They believe that it causes diarrhea, and hence it is squeezed on the cloth and buried. Tomar, Y.P.S. and Tribhuwan, Robin (2007) have reported similar practice among the Mavchi tribals of Nandurbar district in Maharashtra. It is evident from the above facts that tribals have their own perceptions of human physiology and anatomy, which differ to a great extent from that of modern medical science.

CONCEPT OF THE GROWTH AND DEVELOPMENT OF BONES

Informal interviews with the Thakur and Gond respondents revealed that:

- Mothers milk is best for the growth of an infant's bones.
- Rice and Nachani porridge make bones strong.
- Chicken, Goat's meat, green pigeon's meat, flesh and fat of monitor Lizard hooves of goat and chicken and meat soup contribute in making human bones strong.
- Both the tribes recommend chewing of tender goat bones.
- Bones of teenagers and young people between the ages of 20 to 40 are very strong.
- Bones of old people are weak, their blood is reddish black.
- Degeneration of bones in associated with aging.

CONCLUDING REMARKS

It is evident from the facts reported in this paper, that the beliefs and practices of the Gonds and Thakurs regarding Osteoporosis are different from those of the allopathic interpretation or modern medicine. Gonds and Thakurs are just two of the tribes that were studied by the authors. Maharashtra has 45 tribes and in India there are over 750 tribes. It is necessary to document their belief systems not only regarding osteoporosis but other orthopedic disorders as well.

RECOMMENDATIONS

Given below are few suggestions regarding health education and awareness programmes about osteoporosis and other orthopedic disorders.

1. Educate the medical and paramedical staff of the Primary Health centers sub-centers and Rural Hospitals.
2. Educate traditional medical practitioners among the tribals including shamans, bone setters, midwives and herbalists.
3. Conduct camps to identify patients suffering with osteoporosis in the tribal hamlets.
4. Create awareness in schools and tribal hamlets.
5. Publish booklets and pamphlets with illustrations and diagrams.

REFERENCES

Adams J, Hamblen D 2001. *Outline of Orthopedics*. London: Elsevier Church Hill Livingston.

Caudil W 1955. Applied Anthropology in Kroeber AR (Ed) *Anthropology Today*. Chicago: The University of Chicago Press.

Dawson-Hughes B, Harris SS. Calcium Intake Influences the Association of Protein Intake with Rates of Bone Loss in Elderly Men and Women. *American Journal of Clinical Nutrition* 2002: 75: 773-9.

Foster GM Anderson B 1978. *Medical Anthropology*. New York: John Willy & Sons.

Harner M 1973. *Shamanism & Hallucinogens*. New York: Oxford University Press.

Hughes C 1968. *Ethno Medicine, in International Encyclopedia of Social Sciences*. Vol. 10. New York: Macmillan Company.

Jain NS, Tribhuwan R 1996. *The Mirage of Health and Development*. Pune: Vidyanidhi Publication.

Kurian JC, Tribhuwan R 1990. Traditional Medical Practitioners of the Sahyadri, in *Eastern Anthropologist* Vol. 43(3) Lucknow.

Lieban R 1973. Medical Anthropology in Honigman JJ (Ed.) *Social and Cultural Anthropology*. Chicago: Rand and McNally Company.

Love S 1997. *Dr Susan Love's Hormone Book*. New York: Random House.

Maheshwari J 1993. *Essential Orthopedics*. New Delhi: Mehta Publishers.

Schutlur M 1976. Disease and Curing in a Yagui Community, in *Ethnic Medicine in the Southwest* by Spicer E (Ed.). Arizona: The University Press.

Surya B 1993. *A Short Text book of Orthopedics and Traumatology*. New Delhi: Jaypee Brothers Medical Publishers.

Tomar YPS, Tribhuwan R 2007. *Mavchis: A Lesser Known Tribe of Nandurbar*, Pune: Tribal Research and Training Institute.

Tribhuwan R 1998. *Medical World of Tribals*. New Delhi: Discovery Publishing House.

Tribhuwan R, Gambhir RD 1995. Ethnomedical Pathway: A Conceptual Model in Jain NS and Tribhuwan R (Eds.). *An Overview of Tribal Research Studies*. Pune: Tribal Research and Training Institute.

________. Statistics by Country for Osteoporosis. From www.cureresearch.com/o/osteoporosis/stats-country_printer.htm (Retrieved May 18, 2012)

________. List of Countries by Population. From en.wikipedia.org/wiki/List_of_countries_by_population (Retrieved May 18, 2012)

________. Papua New Guinea. From www.everyculture.com/No-Sa/Papua-New-Guinca.html (Retrieved May 24, 2012)

9

Etiology of Osteoarthritis of Knees
A Cross Cultural Study

WHAT IS OSTEOARTHRITIS ?

Osteoarthritis is the most common form of arthritis of knees. It is defined as a degenerative, non-inflammatory disease of the joint characterised by destruction of articular cartilage and formation of new cartilage at the joint surface and its margin. Most common joints affected in osteoarthritis are weight bearing joints such as knees, hips and ankles of the lower extremity and *trapezio-metacarpel joint* (TMC) of the hands of the upper extremity. Although the exact cause of osteoarthritis is not know but given below are some important factors which play very important role in development of osteoarthritis. These are obesity, Heredity, Occupation involving prolonged standing, sports, injury of the joints and multiple metabolic disorders.

CLINICAL FEATURES

Weight bearing joints like knees, Hips and ankles are affected but the most commonly affected joints is the knee joint. Osteoarthritis is common among the elderly people. one in three people over 60 years of age are affected by this disorder and is rarely seen in younger age group persons.

SIGNS AND SYMPTOMS OF OSTEOARTHRITIS

Some of the most typical symptoms of osteoarthritis are:

- Pain in the affected joints.
- Early morning stiffness.
- Swelling of the affected joints.
- Restriction of joint movements.
- In very advanced cases a patient shows a deformity called *Genu varum* deformity.

INVESTIGATIONS

Most important investigation is the X-ray of the affected joints. some of the characteristics features of this disorder on X-ray are loss of joint space, sclerosis, osteophyts at the joint margin and subchondral cysts.

MRI and CT scan are other important investigations requires if needed.

TREATMENT

1. As such there is no treatment for osteoarthritis of knees but counselling, physiotherapy and reassurance are the only part of treatment in early osteoarthritis of knees.
2. Conservative methods.

   About 50 per cent of the patients respond to conservative treatment which consists of:

   - Reduction of weight
   - Isometric quadriceps strengthening exercises
   - Non-steroidal anti inflammatory drugs
   - Intra articular injections of steroid
   - Physiotherapy
   - Heat therapy
3. Surgical treatment
   - Osteotomy
   - Total knee arthroplasty (TKR)
   - Arthrodesis(less commonly indicated)

Well, given above is the medical interpretation of what Osteoarthritis is, its signs and symptoms, clinical features, causes and treatment. In this chapter an attempt has been made to highlight the etiology of osteoarthritis as perceived by various communities.

Objectives of the Study

The objectives of this chapter are two fields namely:

- To study the origin and cause of osteoarthritis of knee joints as perceived by various communities.
- To explore the traditional treatment for the same

RESEARCH METHODOLOGY

The present study is carried out in five tribal communities namely:

- Katkaris
- Kawar
- Warli
- Mavchi
- Pardhan

The katkaris and warlis are found in westerns Maharashtra, in the konkan region, the Mavchis live in north western part of Maharashtra, in satpuda region, the pardhan are found in north eastern part of Maharashtra in Vidharbha region.

The researchers conducted focussed group discussion with key information from the above mention tribes namely Shamans, Herbalists, bone setters, midwives, elderly persons and patients of osteoarthritis of knees. Since the data was qualitative in nature, it was analysed manually.given below are the major findings.

MAJOR FINDINGS

1. The Local Name

The Warlis and Katkaris of the Western Maharashtra call these disorder by two names namely:

- Gudhgyachya Wati (Arthritis of knee)
- Sandhi Wat (Joint pain)

Interestingly the kanwar, Mavchi and the pardhan too have the above mentioned names for the disease.

2. Awareness about osteoarthritis of the knees

Not a single community (tribe) was aware of the scientific name and cause of the disease. They have their names for the disease.

3. Origin and cause of the disease: An Emic (Insider's) view.

Primary data gathered from the respondents belonging to all the five communities (tribes) revealed following facts regarding the origin and the cause of the disease from an insider's perspective.

Table 9.1: Community (Tribes) wise Etiology of Osteoarthritis

Sr. No.	Tribe (Community)	Etiological Beliefs
1	2	3
1.	**Mavchi**	The Mavchis believe that the fluid in the knee joint called "Vangan" in their dialect, becomes less as one gets older. At times it dries up and hence there is a severe pain in the knees. Reduction of "vangan" also gives rise to stiffness of the knee joints.
2.	**Warli**	The warlis believe that osteoarthritis of the knees joints is caused due to long hours of work in the rice fields, at home in the forest and while managing agriculture and daily wage labour, their hip as well as shoulder joints are affected due to hard physical work.
3.	**Katkari**	The traditional beliefs regarding the origin and cause of "Gudgya cha wat" or joint pain in the knees is caused due to entry of cold air in the knee joints. Hence the joint becomes weak and the blood in it becomes black are the major causes of illness.
4.	**Pardhan**	The Pardhan believe that osteoarthritis of the knee joint is caused due to degeneration of knee bone due to old age and also due to avoiding certain strengthening or nutritious food.

(Contd...)

1	2	3
5.	Kawar	The Kawars believe that the osteoarthritis of the knee is caused due to less or no flow of pure blood to the knee joints. It is caused due to weakening of the knee joints. Hard labour in the fields, at home, at work place was yet another cause attributed to the disease by the Kawars.

Analysis

The researchers restricted themselves to only analysing the perception of the above mentioned five tribes on osteoarthritis of knees only. Some of the major causes of osteoarthritis of the knee joints as revealed by the members of the above mentioned tribes is as below.

- Entry of cold air in the knee joints.
- Reduction of fluid in the knee joints.
- Degeneration of bones of the knees due to old age.
- Long hours of work in the field, at home and place of work.
- Adulthood and old age.
- Less or no flow of pure blood.

Therapy for Osteoarthritis

Table 9.2 prevents tribe wise therapy on osteoarthritis.

Table 9.2: Tribe wise Therapy for Osteoarthritis

Sr. No.	Tribe (Community)	Therapy for Osteoarthritis
1	2	3
1.	Mavchi	The Mavchis use castor oil (Riccinus communes) locally called Diws to massage knee joints as a remedy for osteoarthritis of the knees.
2.	Warli	The Warlis use coconut an Karanj oil to massage knee joints and also cut down or give up excess drinking of toddy.

(Contd...)

1	2	3
3.	Katkari	The Katkaris smoke bidis(cigars) is used as a remedy for osteoarthritis. There is yet another Therapy and that is they heat leaves of "nirgudi" (vitex negundo) and tie them on the knees with a cloth.
4.	Pardhan	Massaging the affected knee joints with mauha (tori) seed oil. Consuming Mauha Flower, curry prepared from tori seeds, meat of lizard monitor, seeds of Terminelia arjuna. Applying electrical or brake oil on the affected knee.
5.	Kawar	Hot fomentation on the affected knee joints Massaging the knee joints with sarso oil (Brasic juncea) consumption of milk, milk products and meat.

CONCLUDING REMARKS

Tribal societies do have their culturally held perception regarding the origin and cause of osteoarthritis of the knee. Depending on the etiological perception of the tribes, their course of treatment takes place. The caste and nomadic societies too have beliefs and practices regarding osteoarthritis of the knee. Efforts must be made to carry out further cross-cultural research. Studies to determine tribe caste and nomadic society wise data, on osteoarthritis of knee, hip and even ankle joints.

10

Physical Disability
Social Stigma and Psychological Trauma

INTRODUCTION

India is a vast country with diverse social, cultural, ethnic and economic background. Despite breakthrough in health services, a number of disabilities continue to appear due to polio, communicable and congenital diseases. Increased industrialization, mechanization, vehicular traffic, leading to locomotors disabilities. (Bhist D.B., & others 1986).

The report of the three committees, under the chairmanship of Dr. D.B. Bhist, recommending uniform set of definitions, authorities for certification, have categorized disability into four types namely:

- Visually handicapped
- Physical handicapped
- Speech & hearing handicapped
- Mental handicapped

Each category of handicapped persons has been further divided into four groups namely, mild, moderate, severe and profound/total. It was decided by this committee that various concessions/benefits would be available only to the moderate, severe and profound/total groups and not to the mild groups. The minimum degree of disability should be 40 per cent, in order to be eligible for any concession/benefit. In fact, these aspects have been brought on administrative record, vide Government of India's Resolution No. 4-2/83-H. W. iii, dated 6th August, 1986.

The recommended definitions are as below:

- **Impairment:** An impairment is a permanent or transitory psychological or anatomical loss and/or abnormality. For example, missing of a bodily part, tissue, organ or mechanism of the body.
- **Functional limitation:** Impairment may cause functional limitations which are partial or total inability to perform those activities necessary for motor, sensory or mental functions within the range and manner of which a human being is normally capable such as walking, lifting loads, seeing, speaking, hearing, reading, writing, counting, taking interest in and making contact with surroundings. A functional limitation may last for a short time a long time, be permanent or reversible.
- **Disability:** Disability is defined as an existing difficulty in performing one or more activities which, in accordance with the subject's age, sex and social role, are generally accepted as essential, basic components of daily living, such as self-care, social relations and economic activity. Depending in part on the duration of the functional limitation, disability may be short-term, long-term or permanent.

Medically, disability is physical impairment and inability to perform physical functions normally. Legally, disability is a permanent injury to body for which the person should or should not be compensated.

Disability can be divided into three periods namely:

1. **Temporary total disability** is that period in which the affected person is totally unable to work, during this time, he may receive orthopedic, ophthalmological, auditory or speech or any other medical treatment.

2. **Temporary partial disability** is that period, when recovery has reached the stage of improvement so that person may begin some kind of gainful occupation.
3. **Permanent disability** applies to permanent damage or loss of use of some part/parts of the body after the stage of maximum improvement from any medical treatment has been reached and the condition is stationary.

The aim of this chapter is unveil people's perceptions, attitudes, beliefs and the stigma that is associated with permanent disability of certain musculo-skeletal disorders.

These disorders include:

- Loss of arm and or its part/parts.
- Loss of leg and or its part/parts
- Loss of functions (paralysis) or arm either from shoulder, from elbow or from wrist downwards.
- Loss of functions (paralysis) of by either from hip, from knee or from ankle downwards.

Stiffness of joints, including shoulder, elbow, wrist and fingers of the arm, and hip, knee and ankle of the leg.

Deformities of the back i.e. forward as well as sideways.

Dwarfism among male adults less than 3 feet and among females less than 2 feet & 9 inches.

Gross Disfigurement of face due to injury or burns.

Permanent deformity due to leprosy.

PHYSICAL BEAUTY AND SOCIETY

As aptly pointed out by Mutatkar R.K. (1979:9) that in every society, there prevails an aesthetic concept of physical beauty. The handsome people are admired by the society as in obvious from the adoration received by the film hero and heroine. The idea of personal body image requires all the limbs of the body in right proportion and having a shape pleasing to the eyes. People thank God on the birth of a normal baby and guard him from black magic by putting on charms around the neck or limbs of the baby.

The Thakurs and Katkaris of Raigad district put a black & yellow bead around the neck of the new born called "Dithmani" – meaning a bead to prevent evil eye.

The Baiga of Chhattisgarh put charmed coin necklace around the neck of the child. Putting a black mark on the forehead or check of a new born is a common practice among the Hindus to prevent evil eye. "Nazar utama" – the ritual of warding off evil eye is yet another practice in India to ward off evil eye. (Tribhuwan Robin, 1998).

Physical beauty, states Mutatkar R.K. (1975:9) is also one of the qualities of God which is adored by human beings. According to Tribhuwan Robin (1998), the Thakurs associate human body as a cosmic symbol, that has good & beautiful form. Hence, diseases such as albinism, polydactyl, cleft lips, deformed body, congenital deformities are believed to be inauspicious.

Infact, Tribhuwan Robin (1998) has stated albinos and congenitally deformed children are believed to be offspring's of the evil spririts Munja & Khais. Chaphekar L.N. (1961) who wrote a monograph on the Thakurs captioned, "The Thakurs of Sahyadri", stated that the albino and congenitally deformed children born to a normal Thakur woman are killed after birth because they are offspring's of the evil spirits.

Their body does not resemble with the divine form of the cosmos. Hence, what belongs to the evil work must go back to the evil world, hence such children are buried with their back facing the sun, symbolizing that they should not come back and trouble the Thakurs.

Mutatkar R.K. (1979) hence says that, obviously, deformity in leprosy would be considered as divine punishment. God is considered the embodiment of all perfections, virtue and bliss including beauty. The Christians believe that man is created by God in his own image. That, the human body is the temple of God. People do have religious beliefs about creation of man by the divine beings and forces.

Citing examples of leprosy patients who develop deformity during their life cycle, Mutatkar R.K. (1979:11) stated that a leprosy patient is driven to a stigmatized status at any period in his life after living a richer life in his social group in which he is born.

In the life of a leprosy patient there is sudden change in his status irrespective of whether he belongs to a particular class, caste or religious group. An untouchable leprosy patient is equally rejected by his group, as a Brahmin patient would be rejected by the Brahmins. The disease of leprosy, thus makes a person most unprivileged in the society Mutatkar R.K (1975:11)

He further states that the leprosy patients are rejected even by their kith and kin. They are physically thrown out of their society into compulsory isolation, where patients from their own brotherhood. In no other disease, brotherhood of disease mates is formed to the extent, as in leprosy. Well, studies by Pathan B.R. (1980) revealed that there is social stigma attached to leprosy.

ORTHOPEDIC DISABILITIES: SOCIAL STIGMA AND PSYCHOLOGICAL TRAUMA

Every normal person desires to be useful to his family, to his group, workmates, boss, and to the society at large. The society equips every person to be useful in some trade. During illness a person gets a status of a patient and is treated accordingly in his family or place of work.

Mutatkar R.K. (1975:11) states that a leprosy patient however is denied any place in the society, he becomes a non-person. He loses his ascribed status of fatherhood, husband hood etc. he also loses his achieved status at the place of his work. The status accorded to him is that of social death, a status which has no roles to perform in the society.

Studies by social scientists have revealed that an AIDS patient too is socially rejected by his colleagues at the place of work; in fact the kith & kin too neglect him and ignore him.

OBJECTIVES

This chapter focuses on two issues of patients suffering from permanent physical disability namely:

- The psychological problems they have been through following the post traumas (injury, accident or amputation, head injury) as it were.
- The social stigma attached to their permanent physical disability.

RESEARCH METHODOLOGY

The present study was carried out in general hospital Gadchiroli. The researchers interviewed 30 indoor patients of physical disability, due to accidents. Besides these 30 patients, the researchers interviewed 10 patients who were physically challenged and had certificates given by the civil surgeon.

Case studies of all the 40 patients were recorded. The qualitative data collected was analyzed manually.

MAJOR FINDINGS

The relatives, family members, and the patients who were victims of accidents and had to go through psychological trauma due to injury and amputation revealed following facts:

Psychological Shock

All the 30 patients (100%) were psychologically shocked to see the bleeding injury due to accident. They were terrified with fear. The data revealed that 70 per cent of them became unconscious.

Being a Physically Challenged

The moment, they came to know that they were amputed of their limbs, first thought that came to their mind that they were classified by their society, family members and community as physically challenged.

That, they have to depend on their parents, spouses, children or relatives for several things, that, people could take advantage of their physical disability and limitation.

The Feeling of Weakness

Almost all stated that they felt weak, after the accident and operation (amputation).

The Fear of being Lonely

Out of the 30 patients interviewed, 6 were unmarried. All the six of them were males and stated that, they may not get married, because of the stigma of being a physically handicapped patient.

Inability to Function Normally

All the 30 (100%) patients stated that, they would be unable to function normally. That he would not be able to work and function as normal human being.

Worried Regarding the Response of the Spouse

Out of the 24 married males, 84 per cent were of the view that their wives will not enjoy their company as physically challenged husbands. A few stated that their spouses may not enjoy romance and sex with them. Some said they may get attracted to someone else. These and several other thoughts worried them.

In the next section of the chapter out of the ten respondents, who were not amputed, we have presented five case studies of physically challenged respondents.

Case Study No. 1

Amputation of Right Arm: My Bad Luck

Aim of the cast study: To unveil the impact of amputation of right arm on the socio-economic life and fate of a youth.

Background: Anil Patru Kulmethe, a male, aged 25, a member of Pardhan tribe, was married to a girl, who died in her pregnancy due to Malaria. Anil lives with his mother who is a widow. He is illiterate.

Course of events: Anil hails from Samda village in Saoli block of Chandrapur district. He worked as a daily wage labourer in a rice dehusking crusher. He would get Rs 175/- per da for 45 days per year. On 5th of January, 2013. Anil was near the dehusking machine, he was putting in husk rice bundles in the machine, while working he lost his balance and his right arm fell into the machine and was cut off into 3 to 4 places damaging his bones very badly. He was immediately rushed to the General Hospital in Gadchiroli. The doctor present tied his wounded arm with cotton and bandage. However, being Saturday, the orthopedic surgeon was unavailable, including the anaesthists. On the 8th of January, 2013 the orthopedic surgeon amputed his right arm which was infected and was stinking badly.

During these four days, Anil had to bear pain and the smell of his infected arm. His old mother too was in grief and shock, because her only son met with such a tragedy. Anil and his old mother suffered severely from the psychological trauma for the first four days.

When the authors interviewed Anil a day after his amputation he said: I am helpless, handicapped (thutta), unfortunate and psychologically troubled. I will not be able to use my right hand for eating, drinking water, washing, bathing and for doing several things.

No one will give me a job. My employer paid Rs 5000/- for transportation, medicine, blood, food and hospitalization, but what about financial compensation?

My mother had arranged second wedding with a girl from Chamorshi, who has refused to get married to me after my right arm, was amputed.

What will happen to me, after my mother dies?

Where will I work?

I am socially stigmatized as a handicapped (Thutta) person.

My social interactions will be limited. These and several other questions are troubling Anil mentally.

Anil's hope is his employer, who should give him financial compensation or for that matter some job, so that he and his mother survives.

Analysis

Several socio-cultural and economic issues cropped up after the accident and amputation of Anil's right arm.

These issues are:

Social and economic insecurity. Psychological problems both for him and his old mother. He will have to remain as a bachelor throughout his remaining life. No marriage means, no children. No children means no continuity of lineage. He was socially stigmatized as a physically challenged individual. His house hold, personal and other works were limited due to amputation.Amputation of his right arm was his bad luck.

Case Study No. 2

From Cash to Kind

Aim of the case study: To study the occupational shift as a result of amputation of left arm.

Background: Ravindra Naktu Chichghare, a male, aged 35, a member of another backward community, resident of Chamorshi, District Galchiroli. He is illiterate and currently working as a herder (Gawari) for Karkapalli village, in Chamorshi block. He is married with 3 kids.

Course of events: Ravindra fell from a tree while cutting a big log of wood., and broke his left arm badly. He fell unconscious and was rushed to the General Hospital Gadchisroli in 2004. On examination of th status of his arm, the orthopedic surgeon decided to amputate his arm.

Ravindra, his wife who is illiterate, his daughter Jayshree aged 12, studying in VIIth grade, his son Sujit studying in grade I and Nilesh another son aged six and who is illiterate were psychologically shocked after they saw him with the amputed arm.

Before his arm was amputed Ravindra worked as a daily wage labourer and earned 1000/- per month along with his wife. On an average the family earned Rs 12,000/- per year. However, with amputation the economic, social and psychological scenario of the family drastically changed.

Analysis: Ravindra stopped working as a daily wage labourer. The villagers of Karkapalli offered him a job of rearing their cattle. He no longer gets cash, but gets rice with husk for taking care of 50 cows and bulls. He gets 250 to 300 kilograms of rice with husk for the whole year. He sells rice worth 3000 to 4000 rupees to get cash. Amputation of his left hand has not only caused several psychological problems to

Ravindra and his family members, but he was forced to gain rice with husk in kind, rather than working as a daily wage labourer for cash. Amputation of his left hand not only made him a victim of social stigma but economically he was shifted from cash to kind transaction.

Case Study No. 3

I am deprived of job and marriage due to my physically disabled status

Aim of the case study: To study the impact of physically disabled status depriving an educated girl of job as well as marriage.

Background: Sangamitra, an unmarried female, aged 30, an educated girl with a Masters degree in Sociology and another degree in Bachelor of Education, a member of Teli Caste, is pursuing her second masters degree in History. Her father owns 2 acres of agriculture land and is a farmer. Her mother is a house wife. She has 3 brothers and one younger sister. No one in her family is physically disabled, except for Sangamitra. The family belongs to Teli caste. The average annual income of the family is 20,000/- per annum.

Course of events: Sangamitra is suffering from a congenital musculo-skeletal disorder called "Congenital Talipes Equino varus". It is a disorder as well. She says my parents told me this disorder is not genetic disorder. The left leg became crooked and lifeless when I was 2 years old. She had fever for 7 days. This fever was an abnormal one. It was during this time that, I developed this disorder.

Sangamitra stated that she was asked to get married by my parents to a handicapped boy who is unemployed. However, I refused to get married, because for me getting a job is more important for my social and economic safety. It is unfortunate that I have not been able to get a job despite of my qualification.

Since I did not get a job I am not able to get married. Sometimes I feel no one will marry me because I am 30 years old. My sister Sheela who is younger to me, but is normal got married before me.

Analysis: physically disabled status of this patient deprived her of getting a job and get married too. she and her family members toiled hard to go to many schools and colleges, but failed to find a job, despite of being qualified. Her only hope is completion of her second masters in History, after which she hopes to get a job.

Case Study No. 4

I am dependent on my nephew

Aim of the case study: To explore why orphan physically disabled people have to depend on relatives for survival.

Background: Kondu Durga Boga, a male, aged 29, a member of Gond tribe and a resident of Kosmi village of Korchi block of Gadchiroli district was admitted in the General Hospital for operation of his left leg. Kondy does not have a brother, his 3 sisters are married. His father and mother expired a few years ago. Kondu is living in his house with his nephew's family. Kondu is unmarried because he is physically disabled since birth. He is suffering from "Congenital Talipes Equino Varus" of both the legs since birth. He cannot work normally. The Panchayat Samiti Korchi has given him a wheelchair. He is helped by his nephew to sit on the chair. Kondu owns 2 acres of agriculture land, which is cultivated by his nephew. He has a handicap certificate given to him by the Civil surgeon, General Hospital, Gadchiroli.

Course of events: Kondu is physically disabled due to the congenital deformity he has since birth. He is able to walk very slowly with the help of homemade wooden crutches called "pawada" in Gondi dialect. A physically challenged person is known as "peti paej"in Gondi dialect.

Due to his disabled status Kondu suffered from several psychological problems. He is a victim of social stigma as well as psychological inferiority complex.

When his parents were alive, Kondu expressed the desire of getting married. His desire was however refused by his parents, who said no normal girl will get married to you. Even if she does, she may not live with you. She may elope with another man or may have extra-marital affairs.

He says with his death, his family lineage will cease. I am indebted to my sisters and more importantly my nephew and his wife, who look after me. Thank god I have two acres of land, which is the biggest asset, I have for survival. If it were not for my nephew it would have been difficult for me to survive.

Analysis: There are several cases like Kondu, who are dependent on their relatives for moral, psychological, nutritional, health, occupational and physical support. There is a need to create awareness in remote rural and tribal areas among physically disabled personnel regarding the schemes and programmes meant for them.

Case Study No. 5

Living with the Maggots

Aim of the case study: To study the status of a vagabond suffering from ganglion of right leg, infected by maggots, suffering from insanity and left all alone in the General Hospital Gadchiroli for amputation.

Background: Mr. X, aged around 45 years, a male vagabond, suffering from infection of the right leg, infected by maggots, suffering from insanity, without any relatives and friends was admitted on 15th of January, 2013 in the General Hospital, Gadchiroli. He was suffering so badly that he lost his senses, could not talk properly, and was in terrible pain with maggots in the wounds of his right leg. He was brought into the general ward of trauma unit. His leg had a foul odor. The inmate patients of the ward and their relatives were disturbed psychologically because of the foul smell. The patient was not in his senses. He was speaking senseless things.

The orthopedic surgeon attended to this lonely patient without relatives and friends, applied an ointment to de-worm the maggots on 16th, 17th and 18th of January. The patient felt slightly better. However, the decision of amputing his right leg was pending due to legal reasons. There was no one to sign papers on behalf of the patient. The patient was living with infection, pain and maggots that had entered his wounds, flesh and bones.

Course of events: The detailed case history, life history and the illness episode of the patient could not be documented as no friend or relative accompanied the patient. The patient could be a vagabond or thrown out from his village or family. It was a case of socially rejected and dejected patient. It is possible that he may be living with maggots for several days, months or even years. It was up to the hospital authorities to take decision regarding his amputation and treatment.

When the researchers asked the patient his name, he replied "Afzal Khan". When the second question was asked, "since how long are you suffering from this problem. "He shook his head 3-4 times and said since 3 crore years". This was an indication that the patient had lost his psychological balance. That, he was not in a position to reveal anything about his disease and its history.

CONCLUDING REMARKS

Every normal human being desires to be useful to his spouse, children, family, community, society, boss and colleagues. As a physically disabled or challenged person, he get a status of a patient with physical and social limitation. In fact he is stigmatized and branded as physically challenged person. He gets a certificate from the civil surgeon as a physically handicapped person. He therefore feels secluded socially.

The degree of psychological problems and social stigma of course varies from disease to disease. Deformity caused due to leprosy soils the beauty and form of good body. origin and cause of leprosy as interpreted by several societies is often linked with sins, deedy (karma), sins in past birth, wrath of gods and goddesses and hence leprosy patients were out casted. We therefore read about several instances of leprosy colonies, world over. The psychological trauma and social stigma in leprosy was of greater degree, as compared to other disorders or physical deformities. It is recommended, that further research be conducted taking a larger and cross-cultural sample among physically challenged patients.

11

Educating Traditional Bone Setters
An Imperative Need

INTRODUCTION

In the context of medical pluralism, a wide variety of medical specialists both traditional as well as modern co-exist, whose services a patient may avail to. However, within a traditional medical system, different specialists may be available including shamans, bone-setters, herbalists, masseurs, midwives etc.

In his book captioned, "Medical World of Tribal's", Tribhuwan Robin (1998) has put forth definition of types of medical practitioners prevalent in tribal societies. These ethno-medical specialists are as below:

1. **Shaman:** A shaman is a man or woman who has one or more spirits at his/her command, to carry out his/her bidding for good or to cure persons affected by other spirits or other shamans or simply acting on their own violations. (Harner, Michael, 1973: IX)

   A shaman is known by various vernacular names including "Bhoomka", "Bhagat", "Budwa" etc. Female shamans among the Thakur, Warli, Katkari, Koli Mahadev, Koli

Malhar, Koli Dhar, Kokna tribes of Maharashtra are known as "Bhagatins". (Tribhuwan, Robin 1996, 1998)

2. **Bone Setter:** Bone setters provide treatment for mechanical injuries such as sprains, broken bones, swellings, muscular pain etc. Massaging and branding techniques are also part of mechanical therapy. Bone setters do have some knowledge of major bones in the body. They use palpation technique to detect a fracture. They do not see an x-ray of the fractured bone, as the orhtopaedic surgeons do. Hence, the diagnosis of a single or multiple fractures by a traditional bone setter is based on his knowledge acquired on trial and error basis.

3. **Priest:** A priest on the other hand is a religious functionary, whose supernatural authority is bestowed upon him by a cult or an organisation. In contrast to a shaman, he derives his powers directly from the supernatural sources (Hoebel, 1958: 657). In most societies the priest also plays an important role in healing rites. (Tribhuwan Robin and Gambhir R.D. 1995)

4. **Traditional Birth Attendant:** A traditional birth attendant or midwife as stated by Schutlur Mary (1979: 22) is one, who is always a female and is necessarily not a diviner. Her duties are to give advice and medical aid to expectant mothers, to assist in deliveries and to treat illness that may be for the new mother and child. To fulfill her duties a midwife prescribes a few herbal medicine, knows massage techniques and recommends a proper diet for the new mother and child.

   Tribhuwan Robin and Jain N.S. (1996) have stated that in Akrani and Akkalkuwa blocks of Nandurbar district there are male birth attendants among the Bhils.

   A midwife is known by different vernacular names such as dai, suine, huwarki, etc.

5. **Pôtdhari – The Assistant Midwife**

   Among the Thakurs of Raigad district, in Maharashtra, a midwife is assisted by an assistant known as potdhari, who after gaining an experience of 3 to 5 years may become a midwife. (Tribhuwan Robin, 1998)

6. **Herbalist:** A herbalist is one who may or may not use magico-religious elements in herbal therapy. He also advises hi patients on diet to be taken during ill-health. Besides administering herbal medicines, he also administers medicines extracted from animal and mineral sources. (Tribhuwan Robin and Peters Preeti 1993: 21)
   Herbalists are known by different vernacular names such as "Vaidus", "Baigas", "Jadibutiwale" etc.
7. **Masseur:** A masseur is a male or female who provides massage therapy using medicated oils. Among the tribal and rural societies we get to see female masseurs who give massage to the new born and the mother for a period of 10 to 45 days. She is paid in cash or kind for her services. A male masseur usually gives massage to a male patient as a rule. Masseurs are known as "Malishwale".
8. **Mantrik:** A mantrik is a specialized herbalist, who treats one or two diseases. They also take care of scorpion stings and snake bites. (Tribhuwan Robin, 1998)

All these medical specialists are looked upon with respect by their community members for their skill, knowledge and of course for the health services they render. However, most ethno-medical specialists in rural and tribal societies are not full time practitioners. They are dependent on other economic activities for their livelihood. Qualification for folk medical roles vary considerably. In some cases formal training is required for the practitioners (Metzger and Williams, 1963). In others a long apprenticeship is customary. Given the above background let us look into the nature and role of bone setters.

NATURE AND ROLE OF TRADITIONAL BONE SETTERS

In this section of the book we have discussed following aspects concerning traditional bone setters.

1. Types of Traditional Bone – Setters
2. Procedures for Acquiring Medical Specialty

3. Methods of Diagnosis
4. Medicinal Herbs and Oils Used
5. Techniques of Supporting Fractures Bones
6. Taboos Associated with the Profession
7. Diet Recommended by Traditional Bone Setters

1. Types of Traditional Bone – Setters

Our data has revealed that there are two types of traditional bone setters found in Indian rural and tribal societies, namely:

(a) **Trained:** Trained bone setters are ones, who are exposed to some kind of training in first aid, bone setting, massage, etc by an NGO, orthopaedic surgeon or medical personnel.

(b) **Untrained Bone Setters:** Untrained bone setters are those who are not exposed to any kind of training and base their practice of bone setting entirely on trial and error basis and the traditional knowledge and skills acquired by them through oral tradition.

2. Procedures for acquiring Medical Specialty

The procedure for transferring medical specialty skills as regards the rural and tribal bone setters are concerned, it is observed that the skill is passed on from father to eldest son. Sometimes one or more sons. If a master bone setter does not have a son, he chooses to pass on the skill to his brother's eldest son or an interested trainee of his clan or tribe.

The process of training and apprenticeship is tedious, hectic and long one. The trainee is constantly with the master bone setter. During the course of apprenticeship the trainee acquires following skills:

- Gains knowledge of the position of main bones of the skeletal system.
- Types and nature of fractures.
- The art of fixing bones.
- The different types of herbal medicines used to treat the fractures.

- Medicated oils used for massage, including the technique of massage.
- The skill of branding techniques.
- The skill of diagnosing fractures using palpation method.

3. Methods of Diagnosis

The traditional bone setters diagnose a fracture by:

- Looking at the swelling and position of the damaged bones.
- Using palpation technique.
- Pressing the affected point.
- By observing the swollen area or the fractured bone.
- By examining the pulse, using nadi pariksha.

4. Medicinal Herbs and Oils Used

(a) Tribhuwan Robin (1998) has reported that the Thakurs of Raigad district in Maharashtra state apply the latex of Mauha tree (Madluca Indica) which is applied after setting the fracture. On the latex crushed powder of Nagli Millets (Eleucine coracana) are applied to give a cooling effect. Then, the bone setters tie the set bone with a cloth firmly and leave it for a month for the fractured bones to join naturally. If needed bamboo strips are tied around the set bone to give it support.

(b) The bone setter of Thane Gaon, in Armori block of Gadchiroli district, who is not a tribal, but belongs to Teli caste, applies Jawas oil, on the set bone, wraps a pack of cotton on which Jawas oil is applied and then ties the set bone with a crape bandage firmly. If needed, he uses cardboard strips to support the fractured bone.

(c) The Thakur's, Warli's, Katkari's, Koli Mahadev, Koli Malhar, Koli Dhor, and the Kokna of Western Maharashtra tie hot leaves of Nirgudi (Vitex Negundo) on the set bone for speedy recovery. This therapy is also used for healing joint pains.

(d) The Gonds of Pendra block in Bilaspur district of Chhattisgarh mix til oil (Brassica Juncea) in tobacco and Jaiphal (Mystrica fragrans) powder to applied on joint pains.

(e) Crotontiglium a small shrub also known as Jamalgota in Hindi. The seeds of this plant are a source of croton oil, which is used as a stimulant for paralysis and chronic rheumatism by the rural and tribal people of Assam, Bengal and South India. (Pandey B. P. 1978)

(f) The paste of the root of Operculina turpethum, also known as Indian Jalap in English and Nisoth in Hindi, is found all over India. The paste of the root and some bland oil is applied over rheumatic and paralytic parts of the body, by the traditional bone setter and masseurs.

(g) The oil in which garlic (Allium sativum) is fried is a useful for rheumatic pains. (Pandey B. P. 1978)

(h) The oil extracted from the seeds of Pongamia Pinnata (Karanji) is applied by the Thakur and Katkari bone setters on set bones and joint pains as a remedy for healing.

(i) Nutmeg oil (Myristrica Fragrans) is used externally for rheumatism, by the rural and tribal people of Nilgiris, Kerala, Karnataka and West Bengal.

(j) Sarson oil extracted from the seeds of Brassica Campestris is used for massaging joint pains and the entire body in most districts of Vidarbha region, in the state of Maharashtra.

(k) Coconut oil (Cocos Nucifera) is commonly used for body and head massage all over India.

(l) Olive oil (Olea Europaea) is chiefly used as salad and cooking oil. It is externally applied on joint pains, set bones and swollen parts. The oil is also used for massage by bone setters and masseurs.

(m) **Mauha** (Madhuca Indica) oil, which fresh and properly stored is generally greenish – yellow in colour with an offensive odour and disagreeable taste. It has emollient properties and is used by most tribes in India as a remedy for rheumatism skin disease and headache.

(n) **Crocodile oil:** The Phanse Pardhi hunt crocodiles in the months of Pûs (December), Mâgh (January) and Chait (March), when they are generally fat and yield plenty of oil. The flesh is cut into pieces and stewed over slow fire, when it exudes watery oil. This is strained and sold in bottles at a rupee a seer. The oil is used for rheumatism and for neck galls of cattle. The Pardhis do not eat crocodile's flesh. (Russul R.V. and Hiralal R.B. 1993: 369)

(o) **Peafowl and Pattridges:** The Phase – Pardhis believe that the meat and bones of peafowls and pattridges contributes in making human bones and muscles very strong.

(p) **Monitor Lizard's Oil:** The Madia apply the oil extracted from the flesh of monitor lizard on painful joints. The Madia bone setters also apply the same on fractured bones which are set by them. The Madia bone setters also recommend their patients to consume the meat of monitor lizard. The Madia believe that by consuming its meat the human bones and flesh becomes strong.

(q) **Tender Rhizome of Ginger:** The Koli Mahadev tribal bone setters recommend consumption of raw tender rhizome of ginger (Zingibar officinalis) for patients whose bones are set by them. They believe that the consumed rhizome contributes in joining the bones rapidly.

5. Techniques of Supporting Fractures Bones

Some of the most common techniques of supporting fractures bones by the traditional bone setters are:

(a) **Use of bamboo strips:** Use of bamboo strips to support broken bones of the arms and legs is one of the most common techniques used by the bone setters.

After fixing the bone mechanically, they apply herbal medicine or medicated oil on the affected part. Bamboo strips are then, tied around the arm or leg with a cloth or bandage. These bamboo strips along with the cloth or bandage are kept for a period of 20 to 45 days. The human bones have a tendency of joining and healing naturally once they are fixed.

(b) **Use of wheat flour:** Juwari, a traditional bone setter, of Thane Gaon, tahsil Armori district Gadchiroli, belonging to Teli caste, stated that his father, used knitted wheat flour, instead of bamboo strips and cloth, to plaster fractures of the fore arms. The wheat flour would become dry and support broken ulna, radius bones of the arm. However, he also mentioned that this technique of plastering knitted wheat flour would cause irritation to the skin.

(c) **Use of medicated leaf paste:** In case of open fractures some traditional bone setters, after setting the bones, apply a lot of medicated leaf paste around the arm or leg and then tie it with a cloth. The dry leaf paste supports the bones and heals the wound according to them.

(d) **Use of cardboard strips:** Juwari also uses cardboard strips to support the fracture. He first applies oil on the set fracture area, wraps cotton over it, puts cardboard strips and ties them with a thread, before wrapping bandage over it.

(e) **Use of cloth:** Most traditional bone setters in the rural and tribal areas use cloth to wrap around set fractures, because they are unaware of the use of cotton and bandage.

6. Taboos Associated with the Profession

Tribhuwan Robin (1998), (2004), (2003) who worked among the Thakurs, Katkars, Koli Mahadev, Warli, Kokna, Bhil, Pawara tribes found out that there are certain common taboos among the bone setters of these tribes. These taboos are:

- **Lighting a lamp:** They do not eat dinner, unless and until they light a lamp.
- **Discontinue eating when a lamp goes off:** They stop eating if a lamp is put off, while they are having dinner, lunch or even breakfast.
- **Collection of medicine:** They do not let their shadow fall on a medicinal plant, while plucking it.
- **Food prepared by a menstruating woman:** They do not consume food prepared by a menstruating woman.
- If death occurs in the village, they do not eat till the body is buried.
- They fast on solar eclipse.

Given below is a case study of Hema Raoji Shingva documented by Tribhuwan Robin (1998) of a Thakur bone setter.

Case No. 1

1. Personal Information

A.	**Name**	:	Hema Raoji Shingva
B.	**Sex**	:	Male
C.	**Age**	:	85 years
D.	**Marital Status**	:	Married
E.	**Occupation**	:	Farmer
F.	**Education**	:	Nil
G.	**Village Grampanchayat**	:	Shillar Villages
H.	**Hamlet/Wadi**	:	Shilarwadi
I.	**No. of Years of Practice**	:	70 years
J.	**Social Status**	:	Had – Vaidu

2. Procedure of Medical Apprenticeship

Hema's family are traditional bone setters. The knowledge has been passed down from father to son since generations. Hema being the eldest in the family was taught by his father the art of bone-setting. The period of apprenticeship for Hema was almost 30 years until the death of his father. His training included thorough knowledge of anatomy, physiology, techniques of bone-setting, massaging, study of medicinal plants and more important location of various nerves and branding points on the body. He also learnt the cultural taboos of his profession, the rites of collection, preparation and administration of herbs and medicines.

3. Beginning of Career

Hema Raoji Shingva started his career as a bone setter when he was 30 years old and was doing his apprenticeship under his father. Hema's father had a vision in which he was instructed by the 'Sun God' (God of life) that Hema should carry on with the family tradition and thus serve his fellowmen. This vision was publicly announced. Hema was taken by his father to the village God where he (Hema) took an oath that he will abide by the norms, rules and observe the taboos of the profession and that he will use his medical knowledge only for healing and never to harm anyone. He then offered a coconut.

Hema began his career by giving massages to his father's patients who came with the complaints of swellings. He then shifted to branding patients with hot iron rod. The bone setters and their patients believe that the branding therapy ie; placing hot iron rod on severely painful points on the body is very helpful in relieving pain. From branding he then slowly turned his attention to the practice of the technique of bloodletting. Initially the technique of bloodletting was monitored by his father as there is a lot of risk involved in its practice.

Hema next focused on the art of setting bones. Initially he was helped by his father till he had mastered the art. He was quick to learn the administration doses of plant medicine. He also did not face much problem in identifying medicinal herbs used in his profession. The tribals seem to be good students of Systematic and Economy Botany.

4. Reasons for Taking Up the Profession

On enquiring from Hema why did he choose this particular profession, he replied that (Sun God) 'Parmatma' had assigned this duty of serving sick and the suffering to his family and added that God would definitely reward them (his family) for serving his people. He would reward them in heaven (Swarg).

5. Divine Links with the Profession

Bone setting is always fused with mysticism. Religious elements are always part of this mechanical therapy. Rites related to collection, preparation and administration of medicines are always followed and observed. Hema believes that he gets the power to heal from the Sun God. Before touching a patient Hema asks for help from the Sun God and to maintain his healing power he offers a coconut every Thursday to the village God and abides by the norms of his profession.

6. Taboos Associated with the Profession

(a) Unless and until a lamp is lit Hema does not have his dinner

It is believed that with the setting of the Sun the light goes out and darkness prevails, but when a lamp is lit it symbolizes the presence of the Sun and that the Sun God is with him. The lighting of the lamp is thus symbolic of the Sun and its light (Tej) and that it is present with the practitioner. The presence of light is symbolic to divinity and purity. Darkness is evil, it spoils the food and water which the practitioner has to eat. Thus the food is polluted. If the bone-setter consumes food in the darkness, the light of the Sun (Tej) present within him is put off and he is then unable to heal his patients.

(b) He does not consume food prepared by menstruating woman

Menstrual blood symbolizes impurity and social pollution. If a menstruating woman touches the practitioners food, she pollutes is as the blood symbolizes evil. When it flows out her interaction with others spreads evil and hence she is avoided in the menstruating period. If the practitioner consumes the polluted, the healing light (Tej) within him is put off. The Tej is no longer present in his soul (Atma).

(c) If a woman delivers in Hema's house, he does not eat food touched, cooked or served by her.

The Thakur's believe that the effect of the evil menstrual blood within the body of the woman lasts for twelve days after delivery. They believe that menstrual blood which did not flow out for the nine months and nine days of pregnancy is present in her body.

(d) While eating his food, if a lamp is put off Hema stops eating

As soon as the light is put off darkness prevails and takes control of the situation and pollutes the food. If he consumes this food the healing light within his atma may be put off.

(e) If death occurs in the village, Hema does not eat till the body is buried

Death is evil according to Hema and his profession. It spreads darkness over the village. The medical practitioners therefore abstain from eating as death pollutes their food. If this food is consumed it may cause hindrance in their profession. After the burial of the dead body, Hema has a bath and eats food prepared from freshly drawn well water.

(f) On a Solar Eclipse Hema fasts

Solar eclipse (Surya Grihan) according to the Thakurs is a bad omen. They believe that the Sun God is blocked by evil forces 'Spirits of Mangs and Mahars' (caste groups). Due to this blockage the life rays of the Sun do not reach the earth. Whatever light comes to the earth is evil. The darkness (evil effect) pollutes the food. Hence all medical practitioners fast. After the eclipse is over fresh water (Navin pani) is used to prepare fresh food.

(g) Hema abstains from eating food in a wedding

Turmeric is used to cook food at the weddings. Turmeric (halad) according to the Thakurs is symbolic of a woman and is associated with a married woman. A medical practitioner does not consume this food to avoid contact with a woman.

(h) He does not chase a dog away while eating

It is believed that the Sun God takes the form of a dog to test the practitioner's faith. If the practitioner offers food to the dog then he is a true devotee of the Sun God.

(i) On the day of the Solar Eclipse he takes a lighted incense stick and rotates it in an anti clock direction over all the medicinal plants he uses for medicinal purposes

During a solar eclipse darkness prevails because evil forces have blocked the light of the Sun. It is feared that the medicinal plants in his house may lose their power. Thus the Thakur culture has designed ways and means to retain it. The burning incense stick symbolizes the Sun an its life giving rays. On enquiring from Hema why this ritual is performed, he replied that this ritual is performed so that the plants may be peaceful and get the rays of the sun through the incense stick. The smoke from the incense stick neutralizes the evil effect of the Solar eclipse (Grihan).

7. Healing Rituals

(a) Rituals or methods of diagnosis

Hema Shingva uses two methods for diagnosis:

(i) Observation and/or

(ii) Enquiry

(i) Observation

He observes the swellings, fractures and touches various parts of the body and the nerves to gather information about the seriousness of the case.

(ii) Enquiry

Hema enquires from the patient a detailed history of the accident.

(b) Rituals or methods associated with the collection of Herbs

Herbs and animal sources of medicine are ritually collected. Hema does not allow his shadow to fall on the sources of medicines as the shadow blocks the life giving rays of the Sun and the healing power that is being continuously transmitted to the medicinal plants through the light. Shadow (darkness) is a symbol of death in this context.

(c) Rituals or methods associated with the preparation of medicines

Hema does not store prepared medicines. According to the Thakurs plants are living and they have soul (atma) in their roots. If the medicine is prepared and stored its freshness disappears and it is dead and will be ineffective.

Hema prepares the medicine in the presence of the patient/ his relatives. He faces east during the preparation as the east is the direction of life. This action symbolizes the transmission of healing power of the Sun God (creator of life) into the medicine. Hema chants the name of the Sun God. If the relatives of the patient are present they also time to time chant the name of the Sun God. The patient present gets not only physical relief after consuming the medicine but also psychological relief as he is present during the divine situation of preparing the medicine.

(d) Rituals or methods associated with administration of medicines

Both, the practitioner and the patient face the east while the medicine is being administered. During administration the practitioner chants mantras (prayer) asking/requesting God to heal the patient by making the medicine effective (Bhagvana Hya Davyala Gun Yeude).

(e) Therapeutic measures employed

The bone setter makes use of five different therapeutic measures.

(1) Massaging

The bone setter is an expert at healing swellings/complaints of body ache using massage techniques. He makes use of different types of oil. The most popular being oil of Pongamia Pinnata (oil prepared from the fat of monitor – a reptile). He also uses groundnut oil. He also recommends herbal applications for swelling and body aches.

(2) Branding or 'Chocha Dene'

This technique is often used in cases of severe pain. An iron rod is heated and applied to the points of the body where there is severe pain. More than one point may be branded at a time. Problems like severe stomach ache, joints pain, arthritis etc, are treated using this treatment.

(3) Bloodletting

Thakurs believe that diseases such as migraine, headache are a result of accumulation of spoilt blood in the affected part of the forehead. This spoilt blood should be let out. Hence the practitioner recommends that a cut be made on the forehead to let out the spoilt blood or the petiole of the Mango leaf is thrust hard into the nostril of the affected half to let out the blood, or a corrosive fluid of Semicarpus anacardium (Bibva) seed is applied on the affected part of the forehead to remove the spoilt blood.

(4) Bone Setting

First Hema sets the bone with his hands using techniques taught to him. After setting the bone, bamboo sticks are used to support the dislocated or fractured bones which are tied with cloth. For setting the bone he usually recommends external application. One of his commonly used applications is the latex of the 'Mahua' tree (Madhuca Indica) which is applied on the fracture after setting it. On the latex Nagli seeds (Eleucine Coracana) which are semi – ground are applied to give a cooling effect to the site. The Thakurs believe that the sticky nature of the latex joins the bone.

(5) Hot Medication Therapy

Hema also employs and prescribes hot medication therapy to his patients. These include application of hot water bath, hot herbal packs to the swelling.

8. Thanksgiving Rituals or Practices

As a token of appreciation Hema's patients after getting cured given him a coconut. This he ritually offers to the village God as a token of appreciation for his help and success in curing the patient. Hema never accepts cash as it is a taboo to make his profession an income earning means. But appreciation in kind is welcome. He accepts liquor or a feast given to him.

9. Method of Retiring from the Profession

Bone setting as a profession is practiced till the bone setter has strength to handle his patients. He is instructed by the

Sun God through visions and dreams to give up the profession. This is then announced publicly. Before giving up the profession the bone setter sees to it that a younger practitioner is ready. In Hema's case, his three sons are trained bone setters.

10. Symbols and Meanings Associated with the profession

The 'Sun God' is the symbol of healing. All the healing rites associated with bone setting revolve round the sun. The Sun is the centre in the ritual healing associated with bone setting. Thus, this profession is not only mechanical but is fused with divine aspects and is treated as incomplete without the combination of the two.

Every action involved in healing has a symbolic and meaningful connotation. The action of instructing the bone setter through visions and dreams to take up the practice and continue it till old age shows his relation with the divine force 'Sun', uplifts his image in his society. The Thakur culture has historically designed norms which fuse with divine elements thereby imposing certain responsibilities (status and role) that a person must shoulder to maintain the cultural system. In this case norms imposed on medical practitioners fused with divine elements compel him to render health services through their profession.

Facing 'east' (direction of life) while collecting, preparing and administrating the medicine is symbolic to directly inviting the healing power of the Sun to combine with the medicine. The cultural taboos imposed on medical practitioner have been historically designed to ensure his continual service to mankind.

The Thakur society has also designed ways and means to give thanks to the practitioner. Cash is not accepted by the bone setter (cultural/professional taboo). This practice ensures that if the bone setter becomes popular he does not misuse his curing ability. Hence in kind liquor, clothes or feast is given to the bone setter.

Diet Recommended by Traditional Bone Setters

Primary data gathered by the authors and secondary literature reviewed reveals that the traditional bone setters recommend a common diet for growth and healing of normal as well as fractured bones.

1. **Meat:** Meat of rural hens, peacocks, pigeons, partridges, quails, monitor lizard, goats brain and feet, wild boar, deer etc.
2. **Vegetables:** Green leafy vegetables such as spinach, methi, amaranthus etc. Tomatoes, drumsticks, bitter gourd, beet root etc.
3. **Dry Fruits and Nuts:** Dates, peanuts, almonds, coconut, cashew nuts, Ficus glamerata fruit etc.
4. **Cereals and Millets:** Porridge of rice, corn and ragi (Eleucine Coracana).
5. **Pulses:** Sprouted gram, green peas, pigeon peas and soaked udid dal etc.
6. **Fruits:** Papaya, banana and apples.
7. **Milk and Milk Products:** They recommend milk with turmeric powder and one spoon of sugar.
8. **Peanut Jagery:** Some bone setters recommend peanut – jagery.
9. **Mauha Flowers:** Some recommend consumption of Mauha (Madhuca Indica) flowers before having breakfast in the morning.

LIMITATIONS OF TRADITIONAL BONE SETTERS

Focused group discussions with trained and experienced orthopaedic surgeons revealed following limitations of traditional bone setters:

1. **Diagnosis:** They do not use x-rays, MRI reports and reports of radiologists to diagnose the exact type of fracture or musculo-skeletal disorder.
2. **Cannot treat open fractures:** Generally, most traditional bone setters refer a patient with open fracture to a orthopaedic surgeon, because it is difficult for them to heal the same. In times of emergency, especially during

night or odd hours they do give first aid, but refer the patient to the doctor. Many a time, there are chances of infection while treating a open fracture.

3. **Cannot give anesthesia to the patient:** If the fracture is multiple or complicated, they try to fix the fracture without giving anesthesia to the patient. The patient cries in pain.
4. **They cannot administer pain killers or antibiotics:** The traditional bone setters are unaware of pain killers and antibiotics.
5. **They cannot perform surgery:** In case of a complicated fracture that requires surgery, insertion of implants etc, the traditional bone setters are incompetent to perform surgery.
6. **Unaware of locations of arteries, veins, nerves, ligaments etc.**

   Only a trained and experienced orthopaedic surgeon is aware of the location of important veins, arteries, nerves and ligaments. Only he is able to skillfully operate the patient with the help of germ free and scientific conditions in the operation theatre, with the assistance of other medical helpers.

   A traditional bone setter is not a specialist, trained and experienced orthopaedic surgeon and hence cannot operate a patient with injuries and complicated fractures.
7. **Attending patients with head injuries**

   Majority of orthopaedic surgeons, refer cases of head injuries to a Neuro-Surgeon. This fact is not known to traditional bone setters. Of course, majority of traditional bone setter do not handle cases of head injuries. It is pertinent to note at this juncture, that traditional bone setters should be made aware of this fact, that patients with severe head injuries should be compulsorily referred to Neuro-Surgeons.
8. **Cast and plastering techniques**

   One of the major limitations of the traditional bone setters is lack of awareness and training of cast and plastering techniques.

9. **Handling patients who have fixed rods, plates and other implants**

   It was observed that some patients who have undergone surgeries go to the traditional bone setters for treatment. In such cases, the traditional bone setters should not use conservative techniques of pulling the affected bones or try re-fixing the bone etc. He is incompetent to do this without seeing the x-ray or MRI report.

   The traditional bone setter from Thane Gaon of Armori tahsil, in Gadchiroli district, in the state of Maharashtra, does not feeble with patients who have rods, plates, screws and other implants in their body. He applies medicated oil on the affected part and ties the bone with crape bandage.

10. **Cannot recommend exercises**

    It is said that a successful orthopaedic operation depends on how a physiotherapist and the patient make scientific efforts to exercise. The surgeon does 20 per cent of job by carrying out a successful surgery; however, 80 per cent of his success depends on the scientific movements, recommended by trained and experienced physiotherapists, under the supervision of the orthopaedic surgeon. Each orthopaedic or musculo-skeletal disorder has different kind of exercise. The traditional bone setter is unaware of this. Hence, this too is a major limitation of the bone setter.

11. **An orthopaedic surgeon asks a patient to take a x-ray to confirm whether or not the bone has joined/fixed**

    The orthopaedic surgeon confirms whether the bone has joined or is fixed, by taking a second x-ray of the patient after a period of one to three months. He is able to physical show the patient, before and after situation of the fractured bone.

    The traditional bone setter who is unaware of x-rays cannot show his patients, before – after status of the broken/fractured bones. Hence, this is one of the major limitations of the bone setters.

12. **Traditional bone setters are not registered medical practitioners**

    Traditional bone setters are not registered medical practitioners. This is yet another limitation.

13. **They cannot prescribe allopathic medicines**

    Traditional bone setters cannot prescribe allopathic or even ayurvedic or homeopathic medicines.

EDUCATING TRADITIONAL BONE SETTERS: AN IMPERATIVE NEED

The school of thought that supports the main streaming of traditional bone setters, midwives and herbalists in primary health care, rightly argue that:

1. The traditional bone setters, midwives and herbalists have been providing health care services to the tribal and rural masses, since time immemorial, even before the advent of modern medicine.
2. The traditional bone setters provide treatment, to those who cannot afford to pay money nor give something in kind.
3. The rural and tribal folk give something in cash and kind to the traditional bone setters as per the norms of payment.
4. The traditional bone setters, midwives and herbalists reside in the hamlets an villages amongst their fellow tribes men and attend to them anytime of the day or night.
5. Research studies have pointed out that the P.H.C. doctors and even private doctors are not experienced and trained orthopedic experts and hence cannot attend to the needs of people's musculo- skeletal problems and disorders. The PHC staff and doctors mostly are not experienced and trained orthopedic experts and hence cannot attend to the needs of peoples musculo-skeletal disorders. The PHC. Staff and doctors are mostly at the tahsil head quarters and very seldom go to the remote hamlets to attend patients of orthopedic problems.
6. The rural and tribal people respect traditional bone and and have faith in them.

7. There is a common culture belief among the tribal and rural folk that the profession of bone setting, is taken up by a clan to serve people and not make money.
8. In fact the Thakur scheduled tribe of Raigad district believes that shamans, bone setters, herbalists and midwives have been instructed by god and goddess to serve there triben men. (Tribhuwan Robin,1998).
9. When people are cured of a musculo –skeletal disorder, they willingly pay the bone setter or give something kind.
10. Traditional medical practitioner are believed to get healing power from sun or earth or a deity as it were.
11. Most of traditional bone setter, herbalist and midwives use and administer herbal or animal medicines that lives no side effects.
12. People in the tribal and rural areas believe them; because they spend 10-40 years in learning the art & fixity bones, massaging, giving dietary advice etc.
13. Even educated people from urban areas seek treatment from traditional bone setter.
14. The authors of this book have observed that patients taking treatment from orthopedic surgeons, visiting the traditional bone setters for traditional & medical advice.
15. It was also observed that some bone setter refer complicated cases to orthopedic surgeons.

Well, the reasons stated above create a bond between rural & tribal folk and bone setters. The fact however remains that the rural & tribal masses till date, depend on the traditional bone setters for their health services. That, people can offered treatment of the traditional bone setters and to not have money to pay heavy fees of the orthopedic surgeons practicing private hospitals. This means, that there is a need to give a serious thought to educate traditional bone setters and especially their children, who are educated up to higher secondary college or graduate level. We are of the opinion that both illiterate & literate traditional bone setters practicing in remote tribal & rural areas "where there is no doctor", should be educated and trained by the orthopedic experts and surgeons.

In doing so the traditional bone setters will refer complicated cases to hospitals and orthopedic surgeons. Simultaneously efforts should be made to recruit orthopedic surgeons in rural hospitals and civil hospitals. At least, twice a month an orthopedic surgeon or expert must visit a PHC for consultation and treatment. The trauma units in the rural& general hospitals should be equipped with facilities and medical man power.

There is a need to do lot of basic ground work such as:

1. Identifying traditional bone setters in tribal & rural villages and hamlets by carrying out surveys.
2. Conducting research to understand their knowledge, attitude and practice.
3. Preparing village, block, district and state wise directories of traditional bone setters.
4. Developing rapport with them.
5. Studying the positive aspect of their practice and medicines administered by them.
6. Educating & training them, if they have to be assigned some roles considering their limitations in primary Health Care.

SHOULD THE TRADITIONAL BONE SETTERS BE STREAMLINED IN PRIMARY HEALTH CARE ?

Well, this question has been discussed in national and international conferences organized by the World Health Organisation, Medical Anthropologists and Sociologists and various Medical Associations and NGOs.

The debate revolves around two questions namely:

1. Orthopaedic surgeons, who spend a lot of money in gaining experience and degree do not want to work in rural and tribal areas, especially in Government hospitals.
2. Poor people prefer to go to the traditional bone setters as they cannot afford to pay for the heavy fees of private and even Government hospitals.

Government should recruit trained and experienced orthopaedic surgeons in rural hospitals and even in primary health centers, by giving quality facilities and trained medical man-power to serve the poor people and train the traditional bone setters as well.

12

Socio-cultural Aspects of Sickle Cell Physically Handicapped Patients in Vidharbha
A Case Study

WHAT IS SICKLE CELL ANAEMIA ?

According to the Training Module on Sickle Cell Disease for School, Health, Medical Officers, published by the National Rural Health Mission (2012: 7-13), "Sickle cell disease is characterized by the production of a variant haemoglobin and may result in severe life-threatening clinical symptoms. It is characterized by modification in the shape of the red blood cell, at low oxygen tension, from a smooth, donut shape into a crescent or half moon shape.

Sickle cell disease is an auto – somal recessive genetic disease. Individuals who inherit sickle cell genes from both the parents are homozygote's and develop Sickle Cell Disease (SCD), while those who inherit the gene from only on parent have the Sickle Cell Trait (SCT). Those with the trait are carriers, have no symptoms, but can pass on the gene to their offspring.

As this is a genetic disease, the target population for screening and counseling is young adults and children of 1-30 years age group. In addition, all pregnant women, family members of suffers and carriers and symptomatic individuals of all ages are included. Given below is a diagram showing Sickle Cells and normal red blood cells.

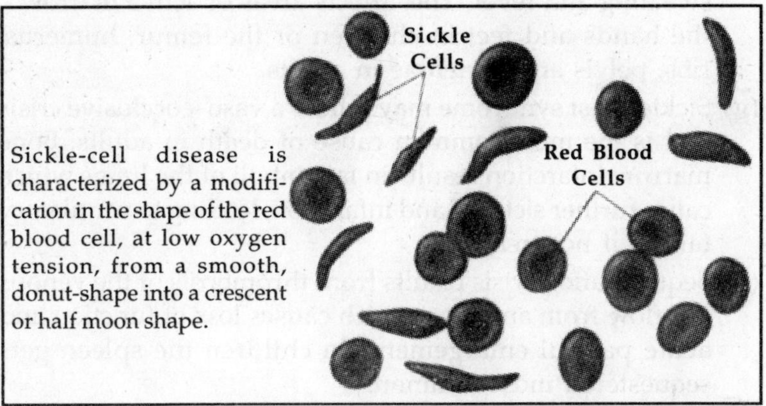

Diagram Showing Normal Red Blood Cells and Sickle Cells

CLINICAL FEATURES OF SICKLE CELL DISEASE

Dr. Sadhana Tayade and Dr. Saranya Singaravel (2012) have presented following clinical features of SCD. These are as below:

(a) SCD has a variable presentation

(b) Sickling is precipitated by:

   (i) Sudden change in temperature.

   (ii) Decrease in oxygenation – high altitude, deep sea diving etc.

   (iii) Infection and fever.

   (iv) Dehydration.

   (v) Acidosis.

(c) Sickled cells have shortened survival, as there is break down of red cells, anaemia and jaundice may be present.

(d) Blockage of blood vessels in the micro – circulation can produce pain.

(e) A number of acute syndromes (crisis) may be seen. Chronic organ damage can also be seen.

(f) The most common type of crisis is the vaso – occlusive crisis. Blockage of small vessels in the bone produces severe bone pain. The heart rate is increased and there is sweating and fever. This affects areas of active marrow – the hands and feet in children or the femur, humerus, ribs, pelvis and vertebrae in adults.

(g) Sickle chest syndrome may follow a vaso – occlusive crisis and is the most common cause of death in adults. Bone marrow infarction results in fat emboli of the lungs which cause further sickling and infarction, leading to ventilatory failure if not treated.

(h) Sequestration crisis results from thrombosis of the venous out flow from an organ which causes loss of function and acute painful enlargement. In children the spleen gets sequestered most commonly.

(i) Aplastic crisis: Infection of adult sicklers with human parvovirus 19 results in a severe but self-limiting red cell aplasia. This produces very low haemoglobin which may cause heart failure. Unlike other sickle crisis, the reticulocyte count is low. Aplastic crisis may also be due to folate deficiency.

(j) Growth and sexual development may be delayed in children.

(k) Infection is a leading cause of death in children with SCD. The signs of infection may include fever, difficulty in breathing, chest pain etc.

(l) Non-healing ulcers may be seen.

(m) Strokes are common in children.

In his book captioned, "Orthopaedic Manifestations and Bone Changes in Sickle Cell Haemoglobinopathy", Babhulkar Sudhir (1997:13) has stated that, persons with sickle cell trait lead relatively normal life, but those with the disease seldom live past forty years and usually present with variety of clinical manifestations i.e.:

1. Fatigue and weakness.
2. Pains in long bones and joints.

3. Pains in hands and feet.
4. Cardiomegaly and systolic murmur.
5. Chronic leg ulcerations and osteomyelitis.
6. Severe abdominal pain and sickling crisis.
7. Icteric sclera and epistaxis.
8. Bone deformities like tower – shaped skull, kyphosis, scoliosis.
9. Spleno/hepatomegaly.
10. Variety of orthopaedic manifestations.

THE EPIDEMIOLOGY OF SICKLE CELL GENE IN INDIA

Sickle cell traits were first reported in India by Lehman and Cutbush (1952) among the aboriginal tribes of South India. Since then it has been reported in tribes of Western India, tribal population of Orissa and Bihar. Workers in tea – gardens in Assam, in the tribal population of Uttar Pradesh and also among the Hindi – Marathi speaking population belonging to low socio-economic group (Mahars, Telis and Kunbis) of Maharashtra in and around Nagpur. (Babhulkar Sudhir 1997:20). Many cases of sickle cell haemoglobinopathies have been reported in India (Dunlop and Mazumdar 1952; Lehman and Cutbush 1952 and Tyagi 1954, R.N. Shukla and B.R. Solank 1958; Kate S. L and others 1995). The concentration of sickle cell is predominantly in Central India.

Research studies have revealed that sickle cell anaemia is prevalent in Vidarbha region of Maharashtra state (Babhulkar 1997; Kate S. L 1995; Urade Bhaskar 2012).

INCIDENCE OF SICKLE CELL DISEASE PATIENTS WITH SKELETAL MANIFESTATIONS AND BONE CHANGES

Dr. Sudhir Babhulkar (1997) detected 7380 patients of sickle cell haemoglobinopathies from 1/1/1970 to 31/12/1995, in various camps and OPDs in Vidarbha region. Out of these 7380 sicklers 944 patients had skeletal manifestations. Approximately 13 to 15 per cent of the total population of sicklers suffer from skeletal manifestations and bone changes.

RESEARCH METHODOLOGY

Universe of the Study

The universe of the present study consisted of 1733 persons, who were suffering from sickle cell disease/trait. Out of these 1733 sickle cell patients 260 were physically handicapped, due to manifestations and bone changes.

These 260, i.e. 15 per cent of the total 1733 number of sickle cell patients were selected as respondent. The sample was selected on the basis of Out Patient Department and medical camp attendance. The table given below depicts the same.

Table 12.1: Nature of Sample Selected

Sr. No.	Sample	Frequency	Percentage
1.	O.P.D. based	142	54.62
2.	Medical camp based	118	45.38
	Total	**260**	**100.00**

As interview schedule was designed to gather quantitative data. Statistical data was analyzed using excel software. Qualitative data was analyzed manually, informal discussion with the parents and spouses relatives of the respondents too were held.

MAJOR FINDINGS

The major findings of the study are as below:

1. **Gender composition**

   Out of the total 260 respondents 125 (48.3%) were males and 135 (51.9%) were females.

2. **Marital status**

   Out of the total 260 respondents 110 (42.3%) were married and 150 (57.7%) were unmarried.

3. **Ethnic and religious status**

   It was observed that 19.2 per cent of the patients were Hindu, 77.7 per cent were Buddhists and 3.1 per cent were Muslims. Interestingly 77.7 per cent of the respondents belonged to scheduled caste.

4. **Type of family**

   61.15 per cent of the respondents belonged to nuclear families, while 33.09 per cent to joint families and 5.76 per cent were single individuals.

5. **Below the poverty line status**

   The data revealed that 92.30 per cent of the respondents were below the poverty line, while 7.70 per cent were non B.P.L.

6. **Knowledge of sickle cell**

   It was observed that 55.76 per cent of the respondents were aware of sickle cell disease 13.76 per cent were unaware and 11.90 per cent did not respond.

7. **Hemoglobin level**

   The study revealed that the hemoglobin percentage was less than 6 grams among 65 per cent of the respondents, above 6 grams and less than 8 grams among 26 per cent of the respondents, more than 8 grams and less than 10 grams among 9 per cent of the respondents.

   It was however observed that not a single respondent H.B. more than 10 grams. This indicates that patients with sickle cell disease were anemic.

8. **Involvement of joints**

   28.85 per cent of the patients had involvement of single joint, 36.92 per cent had involvement of multiple joints and 34.23 per cent did not have involvement of joints. This is one of the most common of sickle cell disease patients.

9. **Nature of physically disability**

   The research revealed that the respondents had following physical disabilities.

10. **Etiology of the disease and bone changes**

    The study revealed that the 260 respondents and their family members had their own perception regard the origin and cause of the bone changes. Informal interviews with patients and their relatives revealed following facts:

    1. Consumption of cows meat.

2. Sexual intercourse with a man or women affected with sickle cell disease.
3. Sins in past birth.
4. Karma (deeds).
5. Bad luck.
6. Entry of sickle cell affecting bacteria and virus into the body.
7. Wrath of gods and goddesses.

Well, given above are socio-cultural beliefs, regarding the etiology of sickle cell disease and bone changes due to the same.

Table 12.2: Nature of Physical Disabilities

Sr. No.	Physical Disability	Frequency	Percentage
1.	Hand-foot syndrome	11	4.2
2.	AVN head of the femur	142	55
3.	AVN head of humorous (shoulder joint)	13	5
4.	Osteomyelitis	19	7.3
5.	Pathological fractures	18	6.9
6.	Growth disturbances	10	3.9
7.	Stiff joints (Hip, Knee)	39	15
8.	Did not respond	08	2.7
	Total	**260**	**100**

CONCLUDING REMARKS

The above data certainly reveals that there is a co-relation between sickle cell disease patient suffering from bone changes and skeletal manifestations and people etiological beliefs regarding the same. 260 handicapped patients interview revealed the socio-cultural aspects associated with the sickle cell disease and the bone changes.

13

Tips on Orthopaedic Treatment and Care

–Dr. Robin D. Tribhuwan
–Dr. Satish S. Meshram
–Ms. Tulika R. Tribhuwan

INTRODUCTION

The subject of Orthopaedics is so vast, scientific and specialized that it us difficult for a common man to comprehend it. Orthopaedic experts spend several years in learning & practical practicing in this field. Even medical doctors who complete M.B.B.S, do not know much about Orthopaedics, as it is not their cup of tea.

A common man gets to know little about Orthopaedics, when he or his family members suffer from a musculo-skeletal disorder, meet with an accident and fracture a bone, or become victim of an injury and so on. The point, which are trying to emphasize at this juncture is that common man has no knowledge of Orthopaedic disorders and its treatment.

TIPS

The authors in this chapter have made an attempt to provide few tips to common people about what basics they should know regarding Orthopaedic treatment. What precautions they should take before & after taking Orthopaedic treatment. Given below are few tips.

1. **Know your skeletal system**

   Most of us study in the schools about our skeletal system, but as time passes by and when we take up other professions and jobs, we tend to forget about the same. We suggest that everyone should get to know not only about the skeletal system, but about main muscles, veins arteries, organs and nerves of our body.

   As regards the skeletal system, it is necessary to know that there are different types of bones in the skeletal system including; long bones, short bones, flat bones, irregular bones & sesamoid bones. That the above types of bones are arranged in two groups namely:

   (a) **Axial** –that contains 80 bones

   (b) **The Appendicular** – that contain 126 bones.

   The bones in the axial skeleton, consists of the skull, the vertebral column, the sternum, the ribs, hyoid & ear ossicles. On the other hand the bones of the appendicular skeleton consist of shoulder girdle, upper extremities, hip girdle and lower extremity.

   Besides the above types of bones, there are joints of the skeleton system. Without joints in between the bones, our whole body would be rigid & immobile. Get to know the different types of joints of the skeletal system. For future reading refer basic books on Orthopaedics.

2. **Read about the basics of fractures**

   These days several books are available that give basic information on definitions & types, of fractures, the dislocation, subluxation, sprain, strain and causes of displacement of fractures etc. Information is available on internet. A common man should learn about the basics of fractures.

3. **Know about the various musculo- skeletal disorders**

   We usually get to know from the doctors about a muscular-skeletal disorder, when we ourselves or any family members become a victim of the same. In the west, people get on the internet to learn more about the disorders. In India, there is less or no awareness about muscular-skeletal disorders, especially among the rural, tribal and nomadic folks. They have their own perceptions of body image, which vary from the scientific interpretation of the anatomy & Physiology of human body. There is a need to create awareness of various musculo skeletal disorders in different languages at school & college level. we advise the patients &their family members to get to know the scientific knowledge about the orthopaedic disorder(s)for which they are getting treatment for.

4. **Explore the exact origin and cause**

   We must make efforts to get to know the exact origin and cause of a given musculo-skeletal disorder, from the orthopaedic surgeon treating a patient, or read about the same.

5. **Opinions of orthopaedic surgeons**

   Take opinions of two to the three renowned & experience Orthopaedic surgeons, before taking decisions on the surgeries. This will help you to confirm, validate and cross check on the Orthopaedic problem faced by the patient.

6. **Cross check treatment cost**

   People are often un aware of the cost regarding surgery, implants, hospitalization, medicine and physiotherapy. It is better to cross check the cost of Orthopaedic treatment before taking the same.

7. **Get to know about the facilities in the hospital and operation theatre**

   Common man is hardly aware, that surgeries carried out in operation theatres which are unhygienic, without sterilized equipments, gowns, and germ free atmosphere can cause infection. Relatives of the patients must make sure that minimum facilities are available in the hospital as well as operation theatre.

   A surgery by the best of the best and most experienced orthopaedic surgeon in an unhygienic operation theatre can spoil the same due to germs & the unhygienic environment or unsterilized equipments. We suggest that people taking, treatment especially those one's getting operated for major surgeries like replacement (hip & knee) and spine surgeries, must check the facilities in the operation theatre.

8. **95 per cent of pediatric age fractures can be managed without surgeries**

   People should know this tact that 95 per cent of the pediatric age fractures can be managed without surgeries conservatively. We have seen doctors in the rural& tribal areas operating children under six years of age. Patents and their relatives are advised to get two to three opinions surgeries of this kind.

9. **Consult a Neuro-surgeon in case of Head Injuries**

   It is recommended that a Neuro-surgeon be consulted in case of serious head injuries for further course of treatment

10. **Significance of physio-therapy**

    Physiotherapy exercises are important and essential, for they help you to get your movement on track. People of then ignore this aspect. It is recommended that a patient & his family members get to know the exact physiotherapy excises and their relevance, with reference to a given musculo-skeletal disorder. Surgery is not only the solution for any fracture, but after an operation is performed physio-therapy plays an important role in healing of the fracture as well as mobilization of joints. If the patient ignores physio-therapy, then the surgery is futile. We have seen patients in rural & tribal areas, who ignored physio-therapy regretted to see their joints being stiff, immobile & deformed.

11. **Be aware of bone-setters**

    We often see people going to bone setters for treatment, because they cannot afford to spend money for orthopaedic treatment in hospitals. We must remember that bone setters have several limitation such as, inability of accurate & scientific diagnosis, diagnosis without x-rays & MRI reports, lack of scientific training, experience & medical degree. An orthopaedic surgeon is aware about the sophisticated investigations, and latest methods available now in orthopaedics. Role of x-rays, MRI and CT scan are very essential

Ebenezar John (2000:23) has summarized the role of x-rays as follows:

(a) X-rays helps confirm the clinical diagnosis.
(b) Helps study the fracture.
(c) Helps study the fracture displacement.
(d) Helps study the crack and stress fracture.
(e) Helps to plan the treatment
(f) Helps to detect fracture dislocation combinations such as Monteggia.
(g) Helps to ascertain post-reduction status of fractures.
(h) Helps in medico- legal studies.

He has also given rules about x-rays. Well, the bone setters do not use x-ray, CT scan or MRI reports to diagnose and hence fail in treating complicated cases. They cannot treat compound fractures. Hence, it is recommended that one should take treatment in a hospital under the supervision and consultation of an orthopedic surgeon.

12. **More degrees less experience**

We come across young orthopedic surgeons, who have degrees from the we stern countries and have bookish knowledge, but have less practical experience in orthopedic surgeries. It is recommended that, it is essential to get know the credentials of theoretical of as well practical experience of an orthopedic surgeon before choosing him for operation and further treatment.

13. **Bone changes in sickle cell disease**

In his book captioned "orthopaedic manifestations and bone changes in sickle cell haemoglobinpathy" (Babhulkar Sudhir 1997:16) has stated that bone changes in sickle cell disease occur mainly because of hyperplasia of bone marrow and because of vascular insufficiency resulting into thrombosis and infarction. Associated bone infection is quite common leading to osteomyelitis and sequestration because of hyperplasia the multiple erythrocyte causes increase in blood viscosity, stasis, capillary thrombosis and finally infarction of bone. The initial infarcts occur in the most distal portion of bone (i.e. femoral head), in the sub chondral area, where there is maximum sick ling & where the circulation through collaterals is very poor.

In addition to the femoral head necrosis, there are changes in other bones also. Changes are seen in long bones, skull, vertebrae, short bones of the hand, ribs and scapulae All these changes are mainly because of hyperplasic born marrow.

Babhulkar sudhir (1997) reviewed & diagnosed 7380 patients with sickle cell disease, out of which 944 that is 13 per cent of patients were with skeletal involvement & had problems of bone changes. A similar study by Meshram Satish (2013) revealed that 14 per cent of the sickle cell disease patients were with bone changes & skeletal deformities.

The point that the authors want bring to the notice of the readers is that there is an incidence of bone changes among patients having sickle cell disease. That, this incidence amounts to 13 to14 per cent of the total number of patients suffering from sickle cell disease.

14. **On Choosing a Ward**

People usually choose a ward hospital, depending on their socio-economic status and the ability to pay the bill for hospitalization, physiotherapy, surgery & medicines. It is recommended, that if the disorder is severe, the patients should be kept in a special or semi-special ward

15. **First aid and Emergency Care of the injured**

First Aid is the initial care of the injured at the scene of accident (Ebenezar John, 2000: 61). Most of us do not bother to read about first aid nor make efforts to learn about the same. Hence in times, of an accident emergency or crisis, we tend to panic. As aptly pointed to by Ebenezar John (2000: 61),' first aid techniques in managing an injured patient should be learnt first and not last. He further states that there is difference between first aid given by a non-medical and medical person. The goals of first aid treatment are:

- Preserve life by carrying out appropriate resuscitative measures
- Prevent further injuries by careful handling.
- Promote recovery.

John Ebenezar (2000) has suggested that following care should be taken initially of the injured at the scene of accident.

- Remove the victim from the accident spot.
- Check his or her vital parameters quickly (pulse, B.P, consciousness etc).
- Seek the help of by standers if trained in firs aid.
- Ensure that police and ambulance have been informed.
- Remember to carry out first Aid according to Mac Murphy's A to F regimen.
- Ensure personal safety

Modus of Operandi in First Aid Air way

First clear the air way as follows:

- Clear the mouth of clots, dentures, loose teeth,.
- Extend the neck slightly as this opens up the pharynx
- If the patient is not breathing, begin artificial respiration. First keep a cloth over the patient's mouth, blow into the patient's mouth keeping his or her nostrils closed. Blow at the rate of 16/minutes and see first the chest raise. Mouth to mouth respiration is carried out if there is extensive injury. If the patient has s extensive facial injuries, put the patient prone. Turn the face to one side and apply pressure over the lower aspect of the chest (Holger-Nelson's method).

Bleeding

It is advisable to arrest bleeding by direct application of pressure over the bleeding points

Cardiac

Examine the radial pulse and the carotid pulse for function of the cardiac; if the pulse is absent the procedure is as follows:

- Ensure that the patient is lying on a hard surface.
- Then pressure is applied with the heel of the palm at the lower end of the sternum.
- Optimum pressure should be applied and depth of each pressure should be1¼ inch.
- Perform external cardiac massage at the rate of 72/ min.
- It is preferable to carry out both external cardiac massage and artificial respiration, Simultaneously by two persons trained in first aid.

Examine the Vital structures

Examine the patient for head, chest, and abdominal spine facial & pelvic injuries.

Remember that delay in first is dangerous. The first one hour span after the accident is known as golden hour, because this period decides the fate of the patient. Managing an accident victim using our knowledge of first aid within the golden hour period can help a patient to survive.

16. **Consult an orthopaedic expert for advise an treatment of Arthritis, osteoporosis, and other orthopaedic Disorders.**

    It is advisable to consult your orthopaedic expert for treatment & care arthritis and osteoporosis and other orthopaedic Disorders.

17. **What is a healthy diet for an arthritic patient ?**

    Interviews with orthopaedic expert and review of literature revealed that healthy diet for an arthritic patient is as below:

    - Include green vegetables, fruits and gram in the diet.

- Control fat cholesterol intake.
- Maintain a healthy weight
- Take the recommended daily requirements of vitamins and mineral including calcium and herbal supplements.

18. **How important is exercise in arthritis**

    Exercise is an important part of treating arthritis. The best Exercise programme for an arthritic patient depends on the type of arthritis he has. The doctor can help the patent to choose an exercise programme to suit his needs patient must consuls an experienced & trained physiotherapist. Exercise contributes in reducing any joint pain and stiffness, increases and develops muscle strength, decreases bone loss, helps control joint swellings, minimizes fatigue and improves sleep, enhances weight lose, keeps the bones and cartilages strong and healthy. Exercises should be carried out under the supervision of a trained physiotherapist.

19. **Orthopaedic expert also recommend yoga, mediation and hydrotherapy.**

    Patents must discuss with their doctors about what yoga, meditation, hydrotherapy and other therapies are good for a given Orthopaedic disorder. Dr. John Ebenezar has recommended yoga exercises for back ache and other musculo-skeletal disorders.

References

1. BabhulkarSudhir, 1997: Orthopaedic Manifestations and Bone Changes in Sickle Cell Haemoglobinopathy, C.B.S Publishers and Distributors, New Delhi.
2. Fabrega, Horacio Jr., 1977: The Scope of Ethno-medical Science, in Cultural Medicine and Psychiatry, Vol. 1, No. 2, pp. 221-228.
3. Hughes Charles, 1968: Ethno-medicine, in International Encyclopaedia of Social Sciences, Vol. No. 10, The Mac Millan Company and Free Press, New York.
4. Harner Michael, 1973: Halucinogens and Shamanism, Oxford University Press, New York.
5. Hoebel E.A., 1958: Man in Primitive World, McGraw Hill Book Company, New York.
6. Lieban Richard, 1973: Medical Anthropology, in Honigman J.J. (ed) A Handbook of Social and Cultural Anthropology, Rand and McNally Company, Chicago.
7. Schutlur Mary, 1976: Disease and Curing in a Yaqui Community, in Ethnic Medicine of the South West (ed) by Spicer Edward, The University of Amazon Press, TUCSON.

8. Matgzer D. and Williams S.G., 1963: Tenejapa Medicine: I the Curer in the South Western Journal of Anthropology, Vol. 15, pp. 216-234.
9. Shah Ira, 2012: Management of Pediatric HIV, (Second Edition) Pediatric on call, Mumbai, India.
10. Bhan Surya, 1993: A Short Textbook of Orthopaedics and Traumatology, Japer Brothers, New Delhi.
11. Kurian J.C. and Tribhuwan Robin, 1990: Traditional Medical Practitioners of the Sahyadri's, in Eastern Anthropologist, Vol. 43, No. 3, July-September Issue, Lucknow.
12. Jain N.S. and Tribhuwan Robin (eds), 1995: An Overview of Tribal Research Studies, TRTI, Pune.
13. Jain N.S. and Tribhuwan Robin, 1996: Mirage of Health and Development, Vidyanidhi Publications, Pune.
14. Tribhuwan Robin and Gambhir R.D., 1995: Ethno-Medical Pathway: A Conceptual Model, in Jain N.S. and Tribhuwan Robin (eds), An Overview of Tribal Research Studies, TRTI, Pune.
15. Tribhuwan Robin, 1998: Medical World of Tribals, Discovery Publishing House, New Delhi.
16. Tribhuwan Robin, 2004: Health of Primitive Tribes, Discovery Publishing House, New Delhi.
17. Tribhuwan Robin and Karen S., 2004: Health Medicine and Nutrition of Tribes, Discovery Publishing House, New Delhi.
18. Tribhuwan Robin and Peters Preeti, 1993: Medico-Ethno biology of the Katkaris and Thakur's in Tribal Research Bulletin, Vol. XIV, No. 1.
19. Tribhuwan Robin and Paranjpe S., 2012: The World of Tribal Children, Balmudra Development and Research Centre, Pune.
20. Tribhuwan Robin and Patil B., 2009: Body Image, Human Reproduction and Birth Control, Discovery Publishing House, New Delhi.

21. Tribhuwan Robin, (ed) Vol. I, 2000: Studies in Tribal, Rural and Urban Development, Discovery Publishing House, New Delhi.
22. Tribhuwan Robin (ed) Vol. II, 2000: Studies in Tribal, Rural and Urban Development, Discovery Publishing House, New Delhi.
23. Tomar Y.P.S. and Tribhuwan Robin, 2007: The Marchis: A Lesser Known Tribe of Nandurbar, TRTI, Pune.
24. Tomar Y.P.S. and Tribhuwan Robin, 2004: Development of Primitive Tribes in Maharashtra, TRTI, Pune.
25. Tribhuwan Robin and Krull Peters, 2004: Die Welt Der Warlis, Druckerei, Krefeld, Germany.
26. TayadeSadhana and Singaravel S., 2012: Training Module on Sickle Cell Disease for School Health Medical Officers, N.R.H.M, Mumbai.
27. Lehman H. and Cut Bush M., 1952: Sickle Cell Trait in Southern India, B.M.J, I: 404.
28. Kate S.L. and Others, 1995: Impact of Genetic Disorders Amongst Tribal Population Groups of Maharshtra, in Jain and Tribhuwan (eds), An Overview of Tribal Research Studies, TRTI, Pune.
29. Urade Bhaskar 2012: Incidence of Sickle Cell Anaemia and Thalessimia in Central India, in Open Journal of Blood Diseases, Vol. 2, pp. 71-80, United Kingdom.
30. Pawar Nicola and Tribhuwan Robin, 2007: Living a Healthy Life: A Case Study of Warli Girl, Vol. 1, TRTI, Pune.
31. Pawar Nicola and Tribhuwan Robin, 2007: Living a Healthy Life: A Case Study of Warli Girl, Vol. 2, TRTI, Pune.
32. Ebnezar John, 2012: Yoga Therapy for Low Backache, C.B.S Publishers and Distributors, New Delhi.
33. Ebnezar John, 2012: Pediatric Orthopedic Problems, (3 Vols.) C.B.S. Publishers and Distributors, New Delhi.
34. Ebnezar John, 2012: Yoga Therapy for Osteoporosis, C.B.S Publishers and Distributors, New Delhi.

35. Young Allan, 1982: The Anthropology of Illness and Sickness, in Annual Reviews of Anthropology, No. 11, pp. 257-285.
36. Sutherland Anne, 1977: The Body as a Social Symbol, in Anthropology of Body (ed) John Blacking, Academic Press, New York.
37. Nitcher and Nitcher, 1981: An Anthropological Approach to Nutrition Education, International Nutrition Communication Service Education Development Centre, 55 Chapel Street, Newton, USA.
38. Newell Kenneth, 1975: Health of People, World Health Organisation, Geneva.
39. Kurian J.C and Bhanu B.V, 1980: Ethno-Medicine: A Study of Nomadic Vaidus of Maharashtra, in the Eastern Anthropologist, Vol.33, No.1, Jan-Mar Issue, pp. 71-78, Lucknow.
40. Hasan K.A. and Prasad B.G., 1959: A Note on the Contributions of Anthropology to Medical Science, in the Journal of Indian Medical Association, 33, 182-190.
41. Hasan K.A., 1967: The Cultural Frontiers and Health in a Village of India, Mankatalas, Bombay.
42. Kumar Abhishek, 2010: Review of Orthopaedics, PeePee Publishers and Distributors, New Delhi.
43. Meshram Satish, 2012: Socio-economic Cultural and Medical Aspects of Sickle Cell Handicapped Persons, an Unpublished Thesis, Social Work Department, Nagpur University, Nagpur.
44. Kumar Abhishek, 2010: Review of Orthopaedics, PeePee Publishers and Distributors, New Delhi.
45. Douglas Mary, 1970: Implicit Meanings (Essays in Anthropolgy), Routledge, Kegan Paul, London.
46. Foster, G.M. and Anderson Barbara, 1978: Medical Anthropology, John Willy and Sons, New York.
47. Foster George, 1983: An Introduction to Ethno-Medicine in Traditional Medicine and Health Coverage, Edited by Bannerman and others, World Health Organisation, Geneva.

48. Turner Victor, 1967: The Forest of Symbols, Ithaca, Cornell University Press.
49. Pandey B.P., 1978: Economic Botany, S. Chand and Company, New Delhi.
50. Koehn D., 1994: The Ground of Professional Ethics, Routledge, London.
51. Hammond Ralph And Wheeler Julie, 2009: The Responsibility of Being a Physiotherapist, in Porter Stuart (ed) Tidy's Physiotherapy, Church Hill Livingstone.
52. Injuries and Violence: The Facts, 2010: World Health Organisation, Geneva, Switzerland.
53. Societal Response to Injury, 2010: World Health Organisation and Education Development Centre, Geneva.
54. World Report on Road Traffic Injury Prevention, 2004: World Health Organisation, Geneva, Switzerland.
55. Mock C.N., et.al, 1998: The Journal of Trauma, Issue No. 44, pp. 804-814.
56. Ebnezar John, 2000: A Text Book of Orthopaedics, Jaypee Brothers, Medical Publishers, New Delhi.
57. Foucault, M. (1967): Madness and Civilization, Tavistock, London.
58. Foucault, M. (1973): The Birth of Clinic, Routledge, London.
59. Foucault, M. (1976): The History of Sexuality, Vol. 1, An Introduction, Penguin, Harmonds Worth.
60. Foucault, M. (1977 a): Discipline and Punish: The Birth of Prison, Penguin, Harmonds Worth.
61. Foucault, M. (1977 b): Nietzsche, Geneology and History, In Language, Counter Memory, Practice edited by D.F. Bouchard, Blackwell Oxford.
62. Foucault, M. (1982): The Subject and Power, In Michael Foucault, Beyond Structuralism and Hermeneutics, Edited by H. Dreyfus and P. Rabinow, Chicago University Press, Chicago.

63. White Kevin, 2011: An Introduction to Sociology of Health and Illness (ed), Sage Publication, New Delhi.
64. Kulkarni S., 2000: Reproductive Health, Status of Married Adolescents as Assessed by NFHS – 2.
65. Park J.E. and Park K., 1991: Text Book of Preventive and Social Medicine, M/s Banarsidas Bhanot Publishers, New Delhi.
66. Madan G.R., 1982: Indian Social Problems, Allied Publishers, Mumbai.
67. Nuland Sherwin, 1988: Doctors: The Bibliography of Medicine Gryphon Editions, Inc, USA.
68. Tribhuwan Robin and Patil Jayshree, 2009: Stone Quarry Workers, Discovery Publishing House, New Delhi.
69. Tribhwan Robin and Jayshree Kharche, 2012: Hard Labour, Poor Pay, in the Published Proceedings of UGC Sponsored, National Conference on Changing Trends in Employment in India, Pragati College, Dombivili.
70. Tribhuwan Robin and Shende Sadashiv, 2012: In the Shade of Searching Labour: A Study of Salt Pan Workers in Kharaghoda, NCCTEI, Pragati College Publication, Dombivili.
71. Breman Jan, 1996: Footloose Labour, Cambridge University Press, Cambridge.
72. Breman Jan, 1994: Wage Hunters and Gatherers, Oxford University Press, New Delhi.
73. Breman Jan and Das Arvind, 2000: Down and Out: Labouring Under Global Capitalism, Oxford University Press, New Delhi.
74. Panjiar Smita, 2007: Locked Homes, Empty Schools, Zubban, New Delhi.
75. Kendre Balaji, 2009: Migration and Development, Unpublished Thesis, Department of Sociology, Shivaji University, Kolhapur.
76. World Health Organisation, 1969: Report of Training Course on Organisation of MCH, Field Practice Programmes in Medical Colleges, SEA/MCH/SC, Dec. 1969, New Delhi.

77. JacoGarthy E. (Ed) 1958: Patients, Physicians and Illness, The Free Press, Glencoe, Illinois.
78. Mutaṭkar, R.K., 1979, Society and Leprosy, Subhada – Saraswati Publishers, Pune.
79. Pathan Babul, 1980, Stigma in Leprosy, Unpublished Ph.D., Thesis, Dept. of Anthropology, University of Pune, Pune -7.

Index